SLOW COOKING

135 MOUTHWATERING RECIPES SHOWN IN OVER 260 PHOTOGRAPHS

CATHERINE ATKINSON

greene&golden

This edition is published by greene&golden,
an imprint of Anness Publishing Ltd, Blaby Road,
Wigston, Leicestershire LE18 4SE; info@anness.com

www.annesspublishing.com

If you like the images in this book and would like to
investigate using them for publishing, promotions or
advertising, please visit www.practicalpictures.com
for more information.

© Anness Publishing Ltd 2012

A CIP catalogue record for this book is available from
the British Library.

Publisher: Joanna Lorenz
Senior Managing Editor: Conor Kilgallon
Recipes: Catherine Atkinson, Jane Bamforth, Alex Barker,
Valerie Barrett, Judy Bastyra, Georgina Campbell,
Jacqueline Clark, Carole Clements, Jan Cutler,
Joanna Farrow, Brian Glover, Nicola Graimes,
Juliet Harbutt, Christine Ingram, Becky Johnson,
Lucy Knox, Biddy White Lennon, Rena Salaman,
Anne Sheasby, Marlene Spieler, Christopher Trotter,
Kate Whiteman, Rosemary Wilkinson, Carol Wilson,
Elizabeth Wolf-Cohen and Jenni Wright
Photography: Karl Adamson, Edward Allwright,
Steve Baxter, Martin Brigdale, Nicki Dowey,
James Duncan, Michelle Garrett, Amanda Heywood,
Janine Hosegood, David King, Don Last,
William Adams-Lingwood, Thomas Odulate,
Craig Robertson, Bridget Sargeson and Sam Stowell
Designed and Edited for Anness Publishing Ltd by
the Bridgewater Book Company Ltd
Production Controller: Wendy Lawson

NOTES

Bracketed terms are intended for American readers.
For all recipes, quantities are given in both metric and
imperial measures and, where appropriate, in standard
cups and spoons. Follow one set of measures, but not
a mixture, because they are not interchangeable.
Standard spoon and cup measures are level. 1 tsp = 5ml,
1 tbsp = 15ml, 1 cup = 250ml/8fl oz.
Australian standard tablespoons are 20ml. Australian
readers should use 3 tsp in place of 1 tbsp for measuring
small quantities.
American pints are 16fl oz/2 cups. American readers
should use 20fl oz/2.5 cups in place of 1 pint when
measuring liquids.
Electric oven temperatures in this book are for
conventional ovens. When using a fan oven, the
temperature will probably need to be reduced by about
10–20°C/20–40°F. Since ovens vary, you should check
with your manufacturer's instruction book for guidance.
The nutritional analysis given for each recipe is calculated
per portion (i.e. serving or item), unless otherwise stated.
If the recipe gives a range, such as Serves 4–6, then the
nutritional analysis will be for the smaller portion size,
i.e. 6 servings. The analysis does not include optional
ingredients, such as salt added to taste.
Medium (US large) eggs are used unless otherwise stated.
Front cover shows sweet pumpkin and peanut curry
– for recipe, see page 141.

PUBLISHER'S NOTE

Contents

Introduction

Long, slow cooking techniques have been used for centuries. From the earliest times, cooks discovered that meat roasted in the dying embers of the fire, or in a pot of gently bubbling stock suspended well above the flames, produced the tenderest results with rich, well-balanced flavours.

THE VERSATILITY OF SLOW COOKING

You will be pleasantly surprised at the range of uses of the slow cooker. Although traditionally associated with cold weather foods, such as warming casseroles, soups and stews, you can also make delicious hot weather dishes, such as chilled patés and terrines, light fish dishes and summery Mediterranean-style pasta meals. The slow cooker really is invaluable when it is warm outside and you don't want to be confined to a steamy kitchen, with the oven pumping out heat. Simply switch on the slow cooker and leave it to it.

THE RISE AND FALL OF THE SLOW COOKER

In the mid-1970s, the slow cooker was invented. It was originally designed for making baked beans and was marketed to the public as an appliance that would cook a wholesome meal unattended, ready to be served after a hard day's work. As such it caught the eye of those with busy lives. It lived up to its promise, and working people and parents soon discovered the advantages of using a slow cooker.

The slow cooker's popularity continued for the next decade. However, with the booming economy years in the late 1980s and late 1990s, the demand for economical cuts of meat fell and also the knowledge of how to cook them disappeared. They were replaced by lean prime cuts, such as chicken breast portions and beef steak, which were more suited to fast cooking methods such as grilling, broiling and stir-frying. Time-saving appliances appeared, including the microwave, and with their arrival, many slow cookers were left to gather dust.

BELOW: *The best type of beef to use for a slow-cooked stew is stewing or chuck steak as the long, gentle cooking tenderizes the meat and brings out the flavour.*

ABOVE: *The gentle heat of the slow cooker means that fish cooks beautifully.*

ABOVE: *Impressive terrines can be made using the slow cooker as a bain-marie.*

ABOVE: *The slow cooker makes excellent steamed chocolate and fruit puddings.*

ADVANTAGES OF USING A SLOW COOKER

Towards the end of the 20th century and in the new millennium, there has been a change in attitudes towards food and a reverse in eating trends. Many people now demand natural food, with fewer artificial chemicals and more nutrients and flavour, rather than instant, quick-fix food. Slow-simmered foods are back in fashion and so is the slow cooker.

Because the slow cooker cooks gently, without the vigorous bubbling or fierce heat of some other cooking methods, delicate food, such as fish, fruit and vegetables, won't break up after long cooking.

There are many advantages to using a slow cooker. Not only does it produce delicious dishes with well-developed flavours, but it uses less electricity than a light bulb, so it can be left unattended, which means you can be away from the kitchen all day and return when ready to serve.

Some slow cookers have timers that automatically switch to the warm setting when the food is cooked. This is ideal for households who eat at different times – the remaining portions of food will still be moist for latecomers, and won't be dry or overcooked. As an added bonus, little steam or smell escapes from slow cookers.

USING THIS BOOK

Ideal for the first-time slow cooker user, who will benefit from the detailed tips and techniques section, this book will also increase the repertoire of the more experienced cook. Most recipes are intended for a family of four people, but if you have a small or large slow cooker the quantities can easily be halved to serve two, or doubled for eight. All recipes have been tested, but it is important to get to know your slow cooker, as times can vary from one model to another.

Soups and appetizers

The slow cooker excels when it comes to soup-making – the long cooking allows the flavours to develop. It is ideal for making appetizers too, particularly pâtés and terrines. This chapter offers dishes for every occasion – from spicy pumpkin soup and seafood chowder for a hearty lunch to Greek avgolemono for an elegant appetizer.

Carrot and coriander soup

The earthy flavour of root vegetables, such as carrots, becomes rich and sweet when cooked slowly over a gentle heat. The flavour goes perfectly with robust herbs and spices.

SERVES 4

450g/1lb carrots, preferably young and tender
15ml/1 tbsp sunflower oil
40g/1¹/₂oz/3 tbsp butter
1 onion, chopped
1 stick celery, plus 2–3 pale leafy tops
2 small potatoes, peeled

900ml/1¹/₂ pints/3³/₄ cups boiling
   vegetable stock
10ml/2 tsp ground coriander
15ml/1 tbsp chopped fresh coriander (cilantro)
150ml/¹/₄ pint/²/₃ cup milk
salt and ground black pepper

1 Trim and peel the carrots and cut into chunks. Heat the oil and 25g/1oz/ 2 tbsp of the butter in a pan and fry the onion over a gentle heat for 3–4 minutes until slightly softened. Do not let it brown.

2 Slice the celery and chop the potatoes, and add them to the onion in the pan. Cook for 2 minutes, then add the carrots and cook for a further 1 minute. Transfer the fried vegetables to the ceramic cooking pot.

3 Pour the boiling vegetable stock over the vegetables, then season with salt and ground black pepper. Cover the pot with the lid and cook on low for 4–5 hours until the vegetables are tender.

4 Reserve 6–8 tiny celery leaves from the leafy tops for the garnish, then finely chop the remaining celery tops. Melt the remaining butter in a large pan and add the ground coriander. Fry for about 1 minute, stirring constantly, until the aromas are released.

5 Reduce the heat under the pan and add the chopped celery tops and fresh coriander. Fry for about 30 seconds, then remove the pan from the heat.

6 Ladle the soup into a food processor or blender and process until smooth, then pour into the pan with the celery tops and coriander. Stir in the milk and heat gently until piping hot. Check the seasoning, then serve garnished with the reserved celery leaves.

Nutritional information per portion: Energy 168Kcal/697kJ; Protein 3g; Carbohydrate 11.9g, of which sugars 9.2g; Fat 12.4g, of which saturates 6g; Cholesterol 24mg; Calcium 94mg; Fibre 3.1g; Sodium 758mg.

French onion soup with cheese croûtes

Probably the most famous of all onion soups, this hearty, warming dish was traditionally served as a sustaining early morning meal to the porters and workers of Les Halles market in Paris.

SERVES 4

40g/1¹⁄₂oz/3 tbsp butter
10ml/2 tsp olive oil
1.2kg/2¹⁄₂lb onions, sliced
5ml/1 tsp caster (superfine) sugar
15ml/1 tbsp plain (all-purpose) flour
15ml/1 tbsp sherry vinegar
30ml/2 tbsp brandy
120ml/4fl oz/¹⁄₂ cup dry white wine
1 litre/1³⁄₄ pints/4 cups boiling stock
5ml/1 tsp chopped fresh thyme
salt and ground black pepper

FOR THE CROÛTES

4 slices day-old French stick, about
   2.5cm/1in thick
1 garlic clove, halved
5ml/1 tsp French mustard
50g/2oz/¹⁄₂ cup grated
   Gruyère cheese

1 Put the butter and oil in the ceramic cooking pot and heat on high for 5 minutes until melted. Add the onions and stir to coat. Cover with the lid, then place a folded dish towel over the top and cook for 2 hours, stirring halfway through.

2 Add the sugar and stir the soup well. Cover with the lid and folded dish towel and continue cooking on high for about 4 hours, stirring occasionally, until the onions are a dark golden colour.

3 Stir in the flour, vinegar, brandy, wine, stock and thyme, and season. Cook on high for 2 hours, or until the onions are very tender.

4 Place the bread under a low grill (broiler) and cook until dry and browned. Rub the bread with the garlic and spread with mustard. Sprinkle over the cheese. Turn the grill to high and cook the croûtes for 2–3 minutes, until the cheese melts. Ladle the soup into warmed bowls and float a croûte on top of each.

Nutritional information per portion: Energy 418Kcal/1747kJ; Protein 11.5g; Carbohydrate 51.8g, of which sugars 19.4g; Fat 15.9g, of which saturates 8.2g; Cholesterol 33mg; Calcium 209mg; Fibre 5.3g; Sodium 1195mg.

Spicy pumpkin soup

This stunning soup has a smooth velvety texture, and a delicate taste, which is subtly spiced with cumin and garlic. Long, slow cooking really gives this soup's flavours time to develop.

SERVES 4

900g/2lb pumpkin, peeled and seeds
  removed
30ml/2 tbsp olive oil
2 leeks, trimmed and sliced
1 garlic clove, crushed
5ml/1 tsp ground ginger
5ml/1 tsp ground cumin
750ml/1¼ pints/3 cups near-boiling
  chicken stock
salt and ground black pepper
60ml/4 tbsp natural (plain) yogurt,
  to serve
coriander (cilantro) leaves, to garnish

1 Using a sharp knife, cut the pumpkin into large chunks. Place the chunks in the ceramic cooking pot.

2 Heat the oil in a large pan and add the leeks and garlic. Cook gently until softened but not coloured.

3 Add the ginger and cumin to the pan and cook, stirring, for a further minute. Tip the mixture into the ceramic cooking pot, pour over the chicken stock and season with salt and black pepper.

4 Cover the slow cooker with the lid, switch to low and cook for 6–8 hours, or until the pumpkin is very tender.

5 Ladle the soup, in batches if necessary, into a food processor or blender and process until smooth. Return the soup to the rinsed out cooking pot, cover and cook on high for 1 hour, or until piping hot. Serve in warmed individual bowls, with a swirl of yogurt and a few coriander leaves.

Nutritional information per portion: Energy 89Kcal/372kJ; Protein 2.3g; Carbohydrate 6.2g, of which sugars 4.7g; Fat 6.3g, of which saturates 1.1g; Cholesterol 0mg; Calcium 75mg; Fibre 3.1g; Sodium 127mg.

Bean and pistou soup

This hearty vegetarian soup is a typical Provençal-style dish, based on beans and richly flavoured with a delicious home-made garlic and fresh basil pistou sauce. For a more substantial meal serve with plenty of fresh crusty bread.

SERVES 6

150g/5oz/scant 1 cup dried haricot
   (navy) beans, soaked overnight
150g/5oz/scant 1 cup dried flageolet or
   cannellini beans, soaked overnight
1 onion, chopped
1.5 litres/2¼ pints/5²⁄₃ cups hot
   vegetable stock
2 carrots, chopped
225g/8oz Savoy cabbage, shredded
1 large potato, about 225g/8oz, diced
225g/8oz French (green) beans, chopped
salt and ground black pepper
basil leaves, to garnish

FOR THE PISTOU

4 garlic cloves
8 large sprigs basil leaves
90ml/6 tbsp olive oil
60ml/4 tbsp freshly grated
Parmesan cheese

1 Drain the soaked haricot and flageolet or cannellini beans and place in a large pan. Cover with fresh cold water, bring to the boil and boil rapidly for 10 minutes, uncovered. Skim the surface.

2 Drain the beans and return to the pan. Add the vegetable stock, onion, carrots, shredded cabbage, chopped potato and French beans to the pan. Season with pepper.

3 Bring to the boil, then transfer to the ceramic cooking pot and switch the slow cooker to high. Cover and cook for 4–5 hours. Season with salt.

4 Meanwhile, place the garlic and basil in a mortar and pound with a pestle, then gradually beat in the oil. Stir in the grated Parmesan. Stir half the pistou into the soup and then ladle into warmed soup bowls. Top each bowl of soup with a spoonful of the remaining pistou and serve garnished with basil.

Nutritional information per portion: Energy 286Kcal/1214kJ; Protein 19.8g; Carbohydrate 50.9g, of which sugars 11.1g; Fat 1.8g, of which saturates 0.3g; Cholesterol 0mg; Calcium 142mg; Fibre 16.1g; Sodium 36mg.

Tomato and fresh basil soup

Peppery, aromatic basil is the perfect partner for sweet, ripe tomatoes – and it is easy to grow at home in a pot on a sunny kitchen windowsill. Make this soup in late summer when fresh tomatoes are at their best and most flavoursome.

SERVES 4

15ml/1 tbsp olive oil
25g/1oz/2 tbsp butter
1 onion, finely chopped
900g/2lb ripe tomatoes, roughly chopped
1 garlic clove, roughly chopped
about 600ml/1 pint/2½ cups
    vegetable stock
120ml/4fl oz/½ cup dry white wine
30ml/2 tbsp sun-dried tomato paste
30ml/2 tbsp shredded fresh basil
150ml/¼ pint/⅔ cup double
    (heavy) cream
salt and ground black pepper
whole basil leaves, to garnish

1 Heat the oil and butter in a large pan until foaming. Add the onion and cook gently for about 5 minutes, stirring, until the onion is softened but not brown, then add the chopped tomatoes and garlic.

2 Add the stock, wine and tomato paste to the pan and stir well. Heat until just below boiling point, then pour the mixture into the ceramic cooking pot.

3 Switch the slow cooker to the high or auto setting, cover with the lid and cook for 1 hour. Leave the slow cooker on auto or switch to low and cook for a further 4–6 hours, until tender.

4 Cool slightly, then ladle into a food processor or blender and process until smooth. Press the soup through a sieve (strainer) into a clean pan.

5 Add the shredded basil and the cream and heat through, stirring. Do not let the soup boil. Check the consistency and add a little more stock if necessary. Season, then pour into bowls and garnish with basil. Serve immediately.

Nutritional information per portion: Energy 335Kcal/1387kJ; Protein 3.1g; Carbohydrate 11.7g, of which sugars 10.8g; Fat 28.9g, of which saturates 16.4g; Cholesterol 65mg; Calcium 50mg; Fibre 3g; Sodium 168mg.

Avgolemono

This light soup is a favourite in Greece and is a fine example of a few carefully chosen ingredients combining to make a delicious dish. It is essential to use a stock that is well flavoured.

SERVES 4

900ml/1¹/₂ pints/3³/₄ cups near-boiling
   chicken stock
50g/2oz/¹/₃ cup easy-cook (converted)
   white rice
3 egg yolks
30–60ml/2–4 tbsp lemon juice
30ml/2 tbsp finely chopped fresh parsley
salt and ground black pepper
lemon slices and parsley sprigs, to garnish

1 Pour the stock into the ceramic cooking pot. Cover with a lid and cook on high for 30 minutes, or until it reaches boiling point.

2 Stir in the rice, cover and cook for 45 minutes, or until the rice is tender. Season to taste with salt and pepper. Switch off the slow cooker, remove the lid and leave to stand for 5 minutes.

3 Meanwhile, whisk the egg yolks in a bowl, then add about 30ml/2 tbsp of the lemon juice, whisking constantly until the mixture is smooth and bubbly. Add a ladleful of the hot soup to the egg mixture, whisking continuously.

4 Slowly add the egg mixture to the soup in the ceramic cooking pot, whisking all the time. The soup will thicken slightly and turn a pretty yellow. Taste and add more lemon juice and seasoning if necessary. Stir in the parsley and serve immediately, garnished with lemon slices and parsley sprigs.

Nutritional information per portion: Energy 98Kcal/410kJ; Protein 3.3g; Carbohydrate 11.1g, of which sugars 0.3g; Fat 4.8g, of which saturates 1.3g; Cholesterol 151mg; Calcium 26mg; Fibre 0.1g; Sodium 211mg.

Lamb and vegetable broth

This is a modern adaptation of the traditional recipe for Irish mutton broth, Brachán caoireola, *and is delicious served with wholemeal bread.*

SERVES 6

675g/1¹/₂lb stewing lamb
2 bay leaves
1 large onion, chopped
3 carrots, chopped
¹/₂ white turnip, diced
¹/₂ small white cabbage, shredded
2 large leeks, thinly sliced
15ml/1 tbsp tomato purée (paste)
30ml/2 tbsp chopped fresh parsley,
    plus extra to garnish
salt and ground black pepper

1 Trim any excess fat from the meat and cut into 2cm/³/₄in cubes. Chop the onion, and put the lamb and bay leaves in a large pan. Add 1.5 litres/ 2¹/₂ pints/6¹/₄ cups water and bring to the boil. Skim the surface and then transfer to the cooking pot. Switch the slow cooker to high.

2 Add the vegetables, tomato purée and parsley, season well and stir together. Cover and cook for 4–6 hours. Ladle into soup bowls and serve garnished with chopped parsley.

Nutritional information per portion: Energy 162Kcal/675kJ; Protein 13.1g; Carbohydrate 8.5g, of which sugars 7g; Fat 8.6g, of which saturates 3.8g; Cholesterol 44mg; Calcium 42mg; Fibre 3g; Sodium 55mg.

Seafood chowder

The word chowder takes its name from the French chaudière *– a pot used for making soups and stews. Like most chowders, this could be served with crusty bread for lunch or supper.*

SERVES 4

25g/1oz/2 tbsp butter
1 small leek, sliced
1 small garlic clove, crushed
1 celery stalk, chopped
2 rindless smoked streaky (fatty) bacon rashers
  (strips), finely chopped
200g/7oz/generous 1 cup canned corn kernels
450ml/³⁄4 pint/scant 2 cups milk
5ml/1 tsp plain (all-purpose) flour
450ml/³⁄4 pint/scant 2 cups boiling
  chicken or vegetable stock

115g/4oz/generous ¹⁄2 cup easy-cook
  (converted) rice
4 large scallops, preferably with corals
115g/4oz white fish fillet, such as monkfish,
  sea bass, cod or haddock
15ml/1 tbsp chopped fresh parsley, plus extra
  to garnish
pinch of cayenne pepper
45ml/3 tbsp single (light) cream (optional)
salt and ground black pepper

1 Melt the butter in a frying pan, add the leek, garlic, celery and bacon and cook, stirring, for 10 minutes, until soft but not browned. Transfer the mixture to the ceramic cooking pot and switch the slow cooker on to high.

2 Place half the drained corn kernels in a food processor or blender. Add about 75ml/2¹⁄2fl oz/¹⁄3 cup of the milk and process until the mixture is blended and fairly thick and creamy.

3 Sprinkle the flour over the leek mixture and stir in. Gradually add the remaining milk, stirring after each addition. Stir in the stock, followed by the corn mixture. Cover the slow cooker with the lid and cook for 2 hours.

4 Add the rice to the pot and cook for 30 minutes. Meanwhile, pull the corals away from the scallops and slice the white flesh into 5mm/¹⁄4in slices. Cut the fish fillet into bitesize chunks.

5 Add the scallops and fish to the chowder and gently stir to combine. Cover and cook for 15 minutes. Stir the corals, parsley and cayenne pepper into the chowder and cook for 5–10 minutes, or until the vegetables, rice and fish are cooked through. Stir in the cream, if using, ladle into bowls, sprinkle with a little chopped parsley and serve immediately.

Nutritional information per portion: Energy 355Kcal/1497kJ; Protein 18.5g; Carbohydrate 45.9g, of which sugars 10.8g; Fat 12.1g, of which saturates 5.8g; Cholesterol 49mg; Calcium 179mg; Fibre 1.5g; Sodium 655mg.

Spinach and root vegetable soup

This is a typical Russian soup, traditionally prepared when the first vegetables of spring appear. You will need to use a large slow cooker to accommodate the spinach.

SERVES 4

1 small turnip, cut into chunks
2 carrots, diced
1 small parsnip, cut into large dice
1 potato, diced
1 onion, chopped
1 garlic clove, finely chopped
¼ celeriac bulb, diced
750ml/1¼ pints/3 cups boiling stock
175g/6oz fresh spinach, roughly chopped
1 small bunch fresh dill, chopped
salt and ground black pepper

FOR THE GARNISH
2 hard-boiled eggs, sliced lengthways
1 lemon, sliced
30ml/2 tbsp fresh parsley and dill

1 Put the turnip, carrots, parsnip, potato, onion, garlic, celeriac and boiling stock into the ceramic cooking pot.

2 Cook on high or auto for 1 hour, then either leave the slow cooker on auto or switch to low and cook for a further 5–6 hours, or until all the vegetables are soft and tender.

3 Stir the spinach into the cooking pot and cook on high for 45 minutes, or until the spinach is tender but still green and leafy. Season with salt and pepper.

4 Stir in the dill, then ladle the soup into warmed bowls and serve garnished with egg, lemon and a sprinkling of fresh parsley and dill.

Nutritional information per portion: Energy 67Kcal/280kJ; Protein 3g; Carbohydrate 11.5g, of which sugars 7g; Fat 1.3g, of which saturates 0.1g; Cholesterol 0mg; Calcium 121mg; Fibre 3.9g; Sodium 499mg.

North African spiced soup

The advantage of cooking soup in the slow cooker is that the flavours have a chance to develop. This technique is particularly well suited to richer soups with complex spicing, such as this one.

SERVES 6

1 large onion, very finely chopped
1 litre/1¾ pints/4 cups near-boiling
    vegetable stock
5ml/1 tsp ground cinnamon
5ml/1 tsp ground turmeric
15ml/1 tbsp grated fresh root ginger
pinch cayenne pepper
2 carrots, finely diced
2 celery sticks, finely diced
400g/14oz can chopped tomatoes
450g/1lb potatoes, finely diced
400g/14oz can chickpeas, drained
5 strands saffron
30ml/2 tbsp chopped fresh coriander
    (cilantro)
15ml/1 tbsp lemon juice
salt and ground black pepper
fried wedges of lemon, to serve (optional)

1 Place the onion in the ceramic cooking pot and add 600ml/ 1 pint/2½ cups of the stock.

2 Switch the slow cooker to high or auto, cover with the lid and cook for about 1 hour, until the onion is soft and translucent.

3 Combine the cinnamon, turmeric, ginger, cayenne and 30ml/2 tbsp of stock, then add to the pot with the carrots, celery and remaining stock. Season. Cover and cook for 1 hour.

4 Add the chopped tomatoes, diced potatoes, drained chickpeas and saffron strands to the pot. Cover and cook for 4–5 hours until all the vegetables are tender.

5 Stir in the chopped fresh coriander and lemon juice then check the seasoning and adjust if necessary.

6 Ladle the soup into individual warmed bowls and serve piping hot, with a few fried wedges of lemon, if you like.

Nutritional information per portion: Energy 166Kcal/705kJ; Protein 7.5g; Carbohydrate 30.3g, of which sugars 7.4g; Fat 2.5g, of which saturates 0.3g; Cholesterol 0mg; Calcium 62mg; Fibre 5.3g; Sodium 335mg.

Chicken soup with knaidlach

This famous Jewish soup is often made using a whole chicken cut into portions and slowly simmered in a huge stockpot. If you have a very large slow cooker you can double the quantities given here, using a small whole chicken; the cooking times will remain the same.

SERVES 4

2 chicken portions, about 275g/10oz each
1 onion, peeled but kept whole
1.2 litres/2 pints/5 cups boiling chicken stock
2 carrots, thickly sliced
2 celery sticks, thickly sliced
1 small parsnip, cut into large chunks
small pinch of ground turmeric
30ml/2 tbsp roughly chopped fresh parsley, plus extra to garnish
15ml/1 tbsp chopped fresh dill
salt and ground black pepper

FOR THE KNAIDLACH

175g/6oz/3/4 cup medium matzo meal
2 eggs, lightly beaten
45ml/3 tbsp vegetable oil
30ml/2 tbsp chopped fresh flat-leaf parsley
1/2 onion, finely grated
pinch of chicken stock cube (optional)
about 90ml/6 tbsp water

1 Put the chicken pieces in the ceramic cooking pot. Cut a small cross in the stem end of the onion and add to the pot with the stock, carrots, celery, parsnip, turmeric, salt and pepper. Cover and cook on high for 1 hour. Skim off the scum that comes to the surface. Cook for a further 3 hours, or until the chicken is tender.

2 Remove the chicken, discard the skin and bones and chop the flesh. Skim the fat off the soup, then return the chicken pieces. Stir in the parsley and dill and continue cooking while you make the knaidlach.

3 Put the matzo meal, eggs, oil, parsley, onion, stock, if using, and water in a bowl and mix to a thick, soft paste. Cover and chill for 30 minutes, until firm.

4 Bring a pan of water to the boil and have a bowl of cold water next to the stove. Dip two tablespoons into the cold water, then take a spoonful of the matzo batter. With wet hands, roll it into a ball, then slip it into the water and reduce the heat to a simmer. Continue with the remaining batter, then cover and cook for 15–20 minutes. Remove the knaidlach from the pan and divide between bowls. Ladle over the soup and serve sprinkled with extra parsley.

Nutritional information per portion: Energy 586Kcal/2451kJ; Protein 38.2g; Carbohydrate 42.6g, of which sugars 6.3g; Fat 30.3g, of which saturates 7.7g; Cholesterol 272mg; Calcium 131mg; Fibre 3.7g; Sodium 802mg.

Genoese minestrone

In the Italian city of Genoa, pesto is stirred into minestrone to add extra flavour and colour. This version is packed with vegetables and makes a great supper dish when served with bread.

SERVES 4

30ml/2 tbsp olive oil
1 onion, finely chopped
2 celery sticks, finely chopped
1 large carrot, finely chopped
1 potato, weighing about 115g/4oz, cut into 1cm/¹/₂in cubes
1 litre/1³/₄ pints/4 cups vegetable stock
75g/3oz green beans, cut into 5cm/2in pieces
1 courgette (zucchini), thinly sliced
2 Italian plum tomatoes, peeled and chopped
200g/7oz can cannellini beans, drained and rinsed

¹/₄ Savoy cabbage, shredded
40g/1¹/₂oz dried "quick-cook" spaghetti or vermicelli, broken into short lengths
salt and ground black pepper

FOR THE PESTO

about 20 fresh basil leaves
1 garlic clove
10ml/2 tsp pine nuts
15ml/1 tbsp freshly grated Parmesan cheese
15ml/1 tbsp freshly grated Pecorino cheese
30ml/2 tbsp olive oil

1 Heat the olive oil in a pan, then add the chopped onion, celery and carrot and cook, stirring, for about 7 minutes, until the vegetables begin to soften.

2 Transfer the fried vegetables to the ceramic cooking pot. Add the potato cubes and vegetable stock, cover and cook on high for 1¹/₂ hours.

3 Add the green beans, courgette, tomatoes and cannellini beans. Cover and cook for 1 hour, then stir in the cabbage and pasta and cook for 20 minutes.

4 Meanwhile, place all the pesto ingredients in a food processor and blend to a smooth sauce. Add 15–45ml/1–3 tbsp water through the feeder tube to loosen the mixture if necessary.

5 Stir 30ml/2 tbsp of the pesto sauce into the soup. Check the seasoning, adding more if necessary. Serve hot, in warmed bowls, with the remaining pesto spooned on top of each serving.

Nutritional information per portion: Energy 263Kcal/1098kJ; Protein 8.5g; Carbohydrate 25.1g, of which sugars 7g; Fat 14.9g, of which saturates 2.8g; Cholesterol 5mg; Calcium 103mg; Fibre 5.4g; Sodium 1034mg.

Cannellini bean soup

From the largest cities to the smallest villages in Greece this soup is a favourite dish. It is always served with bread and olives, and perhaps raw onion quarters or raw garlic for those with robust palates. Pickled or salted fish are also traditional accompaniments.

SERVES 4

275g/10oz/1¹/₂ cups dried cannellini beans,
   soaked overnight in cold water
1 large onion, thinly sliced
1 celery stick, sliced
2 or 3 carrots, sliced
400g/14oz can tomatoes
15ml/1 tbsp tomato purée (paste)

150ml/¹/₄ pint/²/₃ cup extra virgin olive oil
5ml/1 tsp dried oregano
30ml/2 tbsp finely chopped fresh
   flat leaf parsley
salt and ground black pepper
bread and olives, to serve

1 Drain the beans, rinse them under cold water and drain them again. Tip them into a large pan, pour in enough water to cover them and bring to the boil over a medium heat. Cook for about 3 minutes, then drain.

2 Transfer the beans to the ceramic cooking pot, pour in fresh water to cover them by about 3cm/1¹/₄in, then add the sliced onion, celery and carrots, and the tomatoes, and stir in.

3 Add and stir in the tomato purée, extra virgin olive oil and dried oregano. Season to taste with a little freshly ground black pepper, but don't add salt at this stage, as it would toughen the skins of the beans.

4 Cook on high for 1 hour, then lower the heat and cook for about 1¹/₂–2 hours, or until the beans are just tender. Check the seasoning and add salt and pepper to taste, stir in the parsley and serve in warmed bowls, with crusty bread and olives.

Nutritional information per portion: Energy 490Kcal/2,051kJ; Protein 17.9g; Carbohydrate 47.8g, of which sugars 11.3g; Fat 26.6g, of which saturates 4.1g; Cholesterol 0mg; Calcium 89mg; Fibre 8.4g; Sodium 45mg.

Leek and potato soup

This is a hearty Scottish staple, which can be enjoyed as a warming lunch, or a hot drink from a flask by the loch on a cold afternoon. The chopped vegetables produce a chunky soup.

SERVES 4

25g/2oz/2 tbsp butter
2 leeks, chopped
1 small onion, finely chopped
350g/12oz potatoes, diced
900ml/1½ pints/3¾ cups chicken or
    vegetable stock
salt and ground black pepper
chopped fresh parsley, to garnish

1 Heat the butter in a large pan over a medium heat. Add the leeks and onion and cook gently, stirring occasionally, for about 5 minutes, until they are softened but not browned.

2 Add the potatoes to the pan and cook for about 2–3 minutes, then add the stock and bring to the boil. Season to taste.

3 Transfer to the cooking pot and switch the slow cooker to high. Cover and cook for 3–4 hours. Serve hot, garnished with the chopped parsley.

COOK'S TIP
For a different texture, turn the soup into a food processor or blender and process until smooth just before serving.

Nutritional information per portion: Energy 179Kcal/747kJ; Protein 3.2g; Carbohydrate 17.9g, of which sugars 4g; Fat 11g, of which saturates 6.7g; Cholesterol 27mg; Calcium 32mg; Fibre 3g; Sodium 88mg.

Cheese-stuffed pears

These pears, with their scrumptious creamy topping, make a sublime dish when served with salad. If you don't have a large slow cooker, choose short squat pears, so they will fit in a single layer.

SERVES 4

50g/2oz/¼ cup ricotta cheese
50g/2oz/¼ cup dolcelatte cheese
15ml/1 tbsp honey
½ celery stick, finely sliced
8 green olives, pitted and
    roughly chopped
4 dates, stoned and cut into thin strips
pinch of paprika
2 medium barely ripe pears
150ml/¼ pint/⅔ cup apple juice
salad leaves, to serve (optional)

1 Place the ricotta cheese in a bowl and crumble in the dolcelatte. Add the honey, celery, olives, dates and paprika and mix together well until creamy and thoroughly blended.

2 Halve the pears lengthways. Use a melon baller or teaspoon to remove the cores and make a hollow for the filling. Divide the ricotta filling equally between the pears, packing it into the hollow, then arrange the fruit in a single layer in the ceramic cooking pot.

3 Pour the apple juice around the pears, then cover with the lid. Cook on high for 1½–2 hours, or until the fruit is tender.

4 Remove the pears from the slow cooker. If you like, brown them under a hot grill (broiler) for a few minutes. Serve with salad leaves, if you like.

Nutritional information per portion: Energy 236Kcal/992kJ; Protein 6.9g; Carbohydrate 35.6g, of which sugars 35.6g; Fat 8.2g, of which saturates 5.0g; Cholesterol 24mg; Calcium 141mg; Fibre 4.1g; Sodium 261mg.

Haddock and smoked salmon terrine

This substantial terrine makes a superb dish for a summer buffet. It is very good served with dill mayonnaise or a tangy mango salsa instead of the crème fraîche or sour cream.

SERVES 6

15ml/1 tbsp sunflower oil, for greasing
350g/12oz smoked salmon
900g/2lb haddock fillets, skinned
2 eggs, lightly beaten
105ml/7 tbsp low-fat crème fraîche or sour cream
30ml/2 tbsp drained bottled capers

30ml/2 tbsp drained soft green or pink
  peppercorns
salt and ground white pepper
low-fat crème fraîche or sour cream,
  peppercorns, fresh dill and rocket
  (arugula), to serve

1 Pour about 2.5cm/1in of warm water into the cooking pot. Place an upturned saucer or metal pastry ring in the base, then turn the slow cooker on to high. Lightly grease a 1 litre/1¾ pint/4 cup loaf tin (pan) or terrine. Use some of the smoked salmon slices to line the tin, letting them hang over the edge. Reserve the remaining salmon.

2 Cut two long slices of the haddock the length of the tin, and cut the remaining haddock into small pieces. Season.

3 Combine the eggs, crème fraîche, capers and peppercorns in a bowl. Season with salt and pepper, then stir in the small pieces of haddock. Spoon half the mixture into the mould and smooth the surface.

4 Wrap the long haddock fillets in the reserved smoked salmon and lay on top of the fish mixture in the tin. Spoon the rest of the fish mixture into the tin and smooth the surface. Fold over the overhanging pieces of smoked salmon and cover with a double layer of foil.

5 Place the tin in the slow cooker and pour in enough boiling water to come just over halfway up the sides. Cook for 3–4 hours, or until a skewer inserted into the terrine comes out clean. Remove from the slow cooker, but do not remove the foil. Place two or three large heavy cans on the foil to weight it, and leave until cold. Chill for 24 hours.

6 About 1 hour before serving, lift the weights off and remove the foil. Invert the terrine on to a plate and lift off the mould. Slice and serve with crème fraîche, peppercorns, dill and rocket.

Nutritional information per portion: Energy 316Kcal/1326kJ; Protein 46.1g; Carbohydrate 0.4g, of which sugars 0.4g; Fat 14.5g, of which saturates 6.2g; Cholesterol 170mg; Calcium 653mg; Fibre 0g; Sodium 1228mg.

Cardamom chicken mousselines

These light chicken mousselines, served with a tangy tomato vinaigrette, make an elegant appetizer. They should be served warm rather than hot.

SERVES 6

350g/12oz skinless, boneless
    chicken breast portions,
    roughly chopped
1 shallot, finely chopped
115g/4oz/1 cup full-fat soft cheese
1 egg, lightly beaten
2 egg whites
crushed seeds of 2 cardamom pods
60ml/4 tbsp white wine

150ml/¼ pint/²/₃ cup double
    (heavy) cream
oregano sprigs, to serve

FOR THE VINAIGRETTE
350g/12oz ripe tomatoes
10ml/2 tsp balsamic vinegar
30ml/2 tbsp olive oil
salt and ground black pepper

1 Put the chicken and shallot in a food processor and process until smooth. Add the cheese, beaten egg, egg whites, cardamom seeds, wine and seasoning and process until blended. Gradually add the cream, using a pulsing action, until smooth and creamy. Transfer to a bowl and chill for 30 minutes.

2 Prepare six 150ml/¼ pint/²/₃ cup ramekins or dariole moulds, checking that they will fit in the slow cooker. Grease the base of each one, then line. Pour 2cm/³/₄in hot water into the cooking pot and switch the cooker to high. Divide the chicken mixture among the dishes and level the tops. Cover with foil and place in the cooking pot. Pour in a little more near-boiling water to come halfway up the dishes. Cover and cook for 2¹/₂–3 hours until firm.

3 Peel, seed and finely dice the tomatoes and place in a bowl. Sprinkle with vinegar, season with salt and stir. To serve, unmould the dishes on to plates. Put spoonfuls of vinaigrette around each plate, drizzle with oil, season with pepper and add the oregano.

Nutritional information per portion: Energy 191Kcal/795kJ; Protein 18.1g; Carbohydrate 2g, of which sugars 2g; Fat 11.6g, of which saturates 5g; Cholesterol 96mg; Calcium 30mg; Fibre 0.7g; Sodium 130mg.

Chicken and pistachio pâté

This easy version of a classic French charcuterie can be made with white chicken breast portions or a mixture of light and dark meat for a more robust flavour. Serve it as an elegant appetizer for a special dinner, or with salad for a light lunch.

SERVES 8

oil, for greasing
800g/1³⁄₄lb boneless chicken meat
40g/1¹⁄₂oz/³⁄₄ cup fresh white
    breadcrumbs
120ml/4fl oz/¹⁄₂ cup double
    (heavy) cream
1 egg white
4 spring onions (scallions) finely chopped
1 garlic clove, finely chopped

75g/3oz cooked ham, cut into
    small cubes
75g/3oz/¹⁄₂ cup shelled pistachio nuts
30ml/2 tbsp green peppercorns in
    brine, drained
45ml/3 tbsp chopped fresh tarragon
pinch of grated nutmeg
salt and ground black pepper
French bread and salad, to serve

1 Line the base of a 1.2 litre/2 pint/ 5 cup heatproof dish with greaseproof (waxed) paper, then lightly brush the base and sides with oil. Put an upturned saucer or metal pastry ring in the base of the ceramic cooking pot and pour in 2.5cm/1in of hot water. Switch the slow cooker to high.

2 Cut the chicken meat into cubes, then put in a food processor and blend until fairly smooth. (You may need to do this in batches.) Remove any white stringy pieces from the minced (ground) meat.

3 Place the breadcrumbs in a large bowl, pour over the cream and leave to soak.

4 Meanwhile, lightly whisk the egg white with a fork, then add it to the soaked breadcrumbs. Add the minced chicken, spring onions, garlic, ham, pistachio nuts, green peppercorns, tarragon, nutmeg, salt and pepper. Using a wooden spoon or your fingers, mix thoroughly.

5 Spoon the mixture into the prepared dish and cover with foil. Place the dish in the cooking pot and pour a little more boiling water around the dish to come just over halfway up the sides. Cover with the lid and cook for about 4 hours until the pâté is cooked. To check whether the pâté is cooked, pierce with a skewer – the juices should run clear. Lift out of the slow cooker and leave to cool in the dish. Chill in the refrigerator, preferably overnight.

6 To serve, turn out the pâté on to a serving dish and cut into slices. Serve with bread and salad.

Nutritional information per portion: Energy 321Kcal/1344kJ; Protein 36.6g; Carbohydrate 3.7g, of which sugars 1.2g; Fat 17.9g, of which saturates 7.7g; Cholesterol 125mg; Calcium 37mg; Fibre 0.7g; Sodium 379mg.

Red lentil and goat's cheese pâté

The slightly smoky, earthy flavour of red lentils provides a perfect partner to tangy goat's cheese, making a pâté that will be a hit with vegetarians and non-vegetarians alike.

SERVES 8

225g/8oz/1 cup red lentils, rinsed
    and drained
1 shallot, very finely chopped
1 bay leaf
475ml/16fl oz/2 cups near-boiling
    vegetable stock
115g/4oz/¹/₂ cup soft goat's cheese
5ml/1 tsp ground cumin
3 eggs, lightly beaten
salt and ground black pepper
melba toast and rocket (arugula) leaves,
    to serve

1 Place the lentils into the cooking pot and add the shallot, bay leaf and hot stock. Switch the slow cooker to high, cover and cook for 2 hours, or until the liquid has been absorbed and the lentils are soft and pulpy.

2 Turn off the slow cooker. Tip the mixture into a bowl, remove the bay leaf and leave to cool uncovered.

3 Oil and line the base of a 900g/2lb loaf tin. Put an inverted saucer or metal pastry ring in the bottom of the cooking pot. Pour in about 2.5cm/1in of hot water, and switch the slow cooker on to high.

4 Put the goat's cheese in a bowl with the cumin and beat together until soft and creamy. Gradually mix in the eggs until blended. Stir in the lentil mixture and season well.

5 Tip the mixture into the tin. Cover and put in the slow cooker. Pour in enough boiling water to come just over halfway up the sides. Cover and cook for 3–3¹/₂ hours, until just set.

6 Leave the tin on a wire rack until cold. Chill for several hours, or overnight. To serve, turn the pâté out of the tin, peel off the paper and serve with melba toast and rocket.

Nutritional information per portion: Energy 136Kcal/573kJ; Protein 9.8g; Carbohydrate 16g, of which sugars 0.9g; Fat 4.1g, of which saturates 2.6g; Cholesterol 13mg; Calcium 34mg; Fibre 1.4g; Sodium 97mg.

Mushroom and bean pâté

This light and tasty pâté is delicious served on wholemeal toast or with crusty French bread and makes an excellent vegetarian appetizer or light lunch served with salad.

SERVES 8

450g/1lb/6 cups mushrooms, sliced
1 onion, finely chopped
2 garlic cloves, crushed
1 red (bell) pepper, seeded and diced
30ml/2 tbsp vegetable stock
30ml/2 tbsp dry white wine
400g/14oz can red kidney beans, rinsed
    and drained
1 egg, beaten
50g/2oz/1 cup fresh wholemeal
    (whole-wheat) breadcrumbs
10ml/2 tsp chopped fresh thyme
10ml/2 tsp chopped fresh rosemary
salt and ground black pepper
salad leaves, fresh herbs and tomato
    wedges, to garnish

1 Put the mushrooms, onion, garlic, red pepper, stock and wine in the cooking pot. Cover and cook on high for 2 hours, or until the vegetables are almost tender, then set aside for about 10 minutes to cool.

2 Tip the vegetable mixture into a food processor and add the kidney beans and process until smooth.

3 Oil and line a 900g/2lb loaf tin. Put an inverted saucer or metal pastry ring in the bottom of the cooking pot. Pour in about 2.5cm/1in of hot water, and switch the slow cooker on to high.

4 Transfer the mushroom mixture to a bowl. Add the egg, breadcrumbs, herbs, and seasoning. Mix together well, then spoon the mixture into the tin and cover. Put the tin in the slow cooker and pour in enough boiling water to come just over halfway up the sides of the tin. Cover and cook on high for 4 hours, or until lightly set.

5 Place the tin on a wire rack and leave until cold. Refrigerate for several hours. Turn out of the tin, remove the lining paper and serve, garnished with salad leaves, herbs and tomato wedges.

Nutritional information per portion: Energy 85Kcal/358kJ; Protein 5.5g; Carbohydrate 12.3g, of which sugars 3.8g; Fat 1.6g, of which saturates 0.4g; Cholesterol 28mg; Calcium 47mg; Fibre 3.7g; Sodium 187mg.

Fish and shellfish

Delicious, healthy and ideal for cooking

in a slow cooker, fish and shellfish can

be used in a fabulous range of dishes.

The gentle heat of this method cooks the

delicate flesh to perfection every time.

Large whole fish such as salmon will be too

big for the slow cooker, so use small fish,

fish steaks, fillets and shellfish instead.

Baked salt cod with potatoes and olives

Salt cod has been a winter staple in Mediterranean countries for generations. It is also popular during Lent, and is often on the menu at restaurants on Fridays during this time.

SERVES 4

675g/1¹/₂lb salt cod
100ml/3¹/₂fl oz/scant ¹/₂ cup olive oil
800g/1³/₄lb potatoes, cut into
 thin wedges
1 large onion, finely chopped
2 or 3 garlic cloves, chopped
leaves from 1 fresh rosemary sprig
30ml/2 tbsp chopped fresh parsley

400g/14oz can chopped tomatoes
15ml/1 tbsp tomato purée (paste)
about 200ml/7fl oz/scant 1 cup
 boiling water
5ml/1 tsp dried oregano
12 black olives
ground black pepper
chopped fresh parsley, to garnish

1 Soak the cod in cold water overnight, changing the water as often as possible in the course of the evening and during the following morning. The cod does not have to be skinned for this dish, but you may prefer to remove the skin, especially if there is a lot of skin on the fish. You should remove any obvious fins or bones. After soaking, drain the cod and cut it into 4cm/1¹/₂in squares.

2 Heat 60ml/4 tbsp of the oil in a pan. Add the potatoes, onion and garlic and fry for 10 minutes until softened but not browned. Add the rosemary, parsley and plenty of black pepper. Add the remaining olive oil and toss until coated.

3 Add the tomatoes and their juice, the tomato purée and 300ml/¹/₂ pint/1¹/₄ cups water and bring to the boil. Transfer to the cooking pot and switch the slow cooker to low. Stir in the fish and add enough of the boiling water to just cover. Sprinkle the oregano and olives on top. Cover and cook for 7–8 hours. Serve hot or cold, garnished with chopped fresh parsley.

Nutritional information per portion Energy 445kcal/1852kJ; Protein 46g; Carbohydrate 0.4g, of which sugars 0.4g; Fat 27.7g, of which saturates 17.3g; Cholesterol 157mg; Calcium 395mg; Fibre 0g; Sodium 474mg.

Cannelloni Sorrentina-style

There is more than one way of making cannelloni. For this fresh-tasting dish, sheets of cooked lasagne are rolled around a tomato, ricotta and anchovy filling. You can, of course, use traditional cannelloni tubes, if you prefer.

SERVES 4–6

15ml/1 tbsp olive oil, plus extra for greasing
1 small onion, finely chopped
900g/2lb ripe Italian tomatoes, peeled and
    finely chopped
2 garlic cloves, crushed
5ml/1 tsp dried mixed herbs
150ml/¼ pint/⅔ cup vegetable stock
150ml/¼ pint/⅔ cup dry white wine
30ml/2 tbsp sun-dried tomato paste
2.5ml/½ tsp sugar

16 dried lasagne sheets
250g/9oz/generous 1 cup ricotta cheese
130g/4½oz packet mozzarella cheese, drained
    and diced
30ml/2 tbsp shredded fresh basil, plus extra
    basil leaves to garnish
8 bottled anchovy fillets in olive oil, drained and
    halved lengthways
50g/2oz/⅔ cup freshly grated Parmesan cheese
salt and ground black pepper

1 Heat the oil in a pan, add the onion and cook for 5 minutes until softened. Transfer to the cooking pot and switch on to high. Stir in the tomatoes, garlic and herbs. Season, then cover the cooker with the lid and cook for 1 hour.

2 Ladle half of the tomato mixture out of the pot, place in a bowl and leave to cool. Stir the stock, wine, tomato paste and sugar into the tomato mixture remaining in the slow cooker. Cover and cook for 1 hour. Turn off the cooker.

3 Meanwhile, cook the lasagne sheets in batches in a pan of salted boiling water according to the packet instructions. Drain and lay them out on a towel. Add the ricotta and mozzarella to the tomato mixture in the bowl. Stir in the basil and seasoning. Spread a little of the mixture over each sheet. Place an anchovy across each sheet, near to a short end, then roll up into a tube.

4 Transfer the sauce in the cooker to a food processor and purée. Wash and dry the cooking pot, then oil the base and halfway up the sides. Spoon a third of the puréed sauce into the pot, covering the base. Arrange the cannelloni seam-side down on top. Spoon over the remaining sauce. Sprinkle with Parmesan. Cover and cook on high or auto for 1 hour, then switch to low or leave on auto and cook for 1 hour until the cannelloni is tender. Serve with basil.

Nutritional information per portion: Energy 546Kcal/2293kJ; Protein 25.5g; Carbohydrate 54.3g, of which sugars 9.7g; Fat 24.1g, of which saturates 13.4g; Cholesterol 58mg; Calcium 301mg; Fibre 3.5g; Sodium 282mg.

Salmon risotto with cucumber

A classic risotto is time-consuming to make because the stock needs to be added very gradually and requires constant attention from the cook. Here, the wine and stock are added in one go, making it far easier, yet still giving a delicious, creamy texture.

SERVES 4

25g/1oz/2 tbsp butter

small bunch of spring onions (scallions), finely sliced

1/2 cucumber, peeled, seeded and chopped

225g/8oz/generous 1 cup easy-cook (converted) Italian rice

750ml/1¼ pints/3 cups boiling stock

120ml/4fl oz/½ cup white wine

450g/1lb salmon fillet, skinned and diced

45ml/3 tbsp chopped fresh tarragon

salt and ground black pepper

1 Put the butter in the ceramic cooking pot and switch the slow cooker to high. Leave to melt for 15 minutes, then stir in the spring onions and cucumber. Cover and cook for 30 minutes.

2 Add the rice to the pot and stir, then pour in the stock and wine. Cover with the lid and cook for 45 minutes, stirring once halfway through cooking.

3 Stir the diced salmon into the risotto and season with salt and pepper. Cook for a further 15 minutes, or until the rice is tender and the salmon just cooked. Switch off the slow cooker and leave the risotto to stand for 5 minutes.

4 Remove the lid, add the chopped tarragon and mix lightly. Spoon the risotto into individual warmed bowls or plates and serve immediately.

Nutritional information per portion: Energy 506Kcal/2122kJ; Protein 28.4g; Carbohydrate 51.3g, of which sugars 2.8g; Fat 20g, of which saturates 5.9g; Cholesterol 70mg; Calcium 91mg; Fibre 1.4g; Sodium 266mg.

Creamy anchovy and potato bake

This classic Scandinavian dish of potatoes, onions and anchovies cooked with cream makes a hearty winter lunch or simple supper, served with a refreshing salad. In Norway and Sweden, it is often served as a hot appetizer.

SERVES 4

1kg/2¼ lb maincrop potatoes, peeled
25g/1oz/2 tbsp butter
2 onions, cut into rings
2 x 50g/2oz cans anchovy fillets, drained
   reserving 15ml/1 tbsp oil
150ml/¼ pint/⅔ cup single
   (light) cream
150ml/¼ pint/⅔ cup double
   (heavy) cream
15ml/1 tbsp chopped fresh parsley
ground black pepper
fresh crusty bread, to serve

1 Cut the potatoes into slices slightly thicker than 1cm/½in. Cut the slices into strips slightly more than 1cm/½in wide.

2 Use half of the butter to grease the base and sides of the cooking pot, and layer half the potatoes and onions in the base. Cut the anchovies into thin strips and lay over the potatoes and onions, then layer the remaining potatoes and onions on top.

3 Combine the single cream and anchovy oil and season with a little pepper. Pour the mixture over the potatoes and dot with butter.

4 Cover and cook on high for 3½ hours, or until the potatoes and onions are tender. Brown under a hot grill (broiler), if you like, then drizzle over the double cream and sprinkle with parsley and pepper. Serve the bake with lots of fresh crusty bread.

Nutritional information per portion: Energy 378Kcal/1580kJ; Protein 11.3g; Carbohydrate 37.9g, of which sugars 6.4g; Fat 21.2g, of which saturates 11.4g; Cholesterol 54mg; Calcium 1460mg; Fibre 11.5g; Sodium 133mg.

Poached fish in spicy tomato sauce

This traditional Jewish dish is known as **Samak**. *It is usually served with flatbreads, such as pitta or matzos, but you can serve it with plain boiled rice or noodles, if you prefer.*

SERVES 4

15ml/1 tbsp vegetable or olive oil
1 onion, finely chopped
150ml/¼ pint/²/₃ cup passata
    (bottled strained tomatoes)
75ml/2¹/₂fl oz/¹/₃ cup boiling fish
    or vegetable stock
2 garlic cloves, crushed
1 small red chilli, seeded and chopped
pinch of ground ginger
pinch of curry powder
pinch of ground cumin
pinch of ground turmeric
seeds from 1 cardamom pod
juice of 1 lemon, plus extra if needed
900g/2lb mixed firm white fish fillets
30ml/2 tbsp chopped fresh coriander
    (cilantro)
30ml/2 tbsp chopped fresh parsley
salt and ground black pepper

1 Heat the oil in a large frying pan, add the onion and cook gently, stirring, for 10 minutes until soft but not coloured.

2 Transfer the onions to the ceramic cooking pot, then stir in the passata, stock, garlic, chilli, ginger, curry powder, cumin, turmeric, cardamom, lemon juice, salt and black pepper. Cover and cook on high or auto for 1¹/₂ hours, or until the mixture is just simmering.

3 Add the fish to the pot, cover and continue cooking on auto or low for 45 minutes–1 hour, or until the fish is tender. (The flesh should flake easily.)

4 Lift the fish carefully on to warmed serving plates. Stir the chopped fresh coriander and parsley into the sauce, then taste and adjust the seasoning, adding more lemon juice, if necessary. Spoon the sauce over the fish and serve immediately.

Nutritional information per portion: Energy 224Kcal/942kJ; Protein 42g; Carbohydrate 4.1g, of which sugars 3.1g; Fat 4.4g, of which saturates 0.6g; Cholesterol 104mg; Calcium 34mg; Fibre 0.8g; Sodium 151mg.

Coconut salmon

Salmon is quite a robust fish, and responds well to being cooked with this fragrant blend of spices, garlic and chilli. Coconut milk adds a mellow touch and a creamy taste.

SERVES 4

15ml/1 tbsp oil
1 onion, finely chopped
2 fresh green chillies, seeded and chopped
2 garlic cloves, crushed
2.5cm/1in piece fresh root ginger, grated
175ml/6fl oz/3/4 cup coconut milk
10ml/2 tsp ground cumin
5ml/1 tsp ground coriander
4 salmon steaks, each about 175g/6oz
10ml/2 tsp chilli powder
2.5ml/1/2 tsp ground turmeric
15ml/1 tbsp white wine vinegar
1.5ml/1/4 tsp salt
fresh coriander (cilantro) sprigs,
   to garnish
rice tossed with spring onions (scallions),
   to serve

1 Heat the oil in a pan, add the onion, chillies, garlic and ginger and fry for 5–6 minutes, until fairly soft. Place in a food processor with 120ml/4fl oz/ 1/2 cup of the coconut milk and blend until smooth. Tip the paste into the cooking pot.

2 Stir in 5ml/1 tsp of the cumin, the ground coriander and the rest of the coconut milk. Cover and cook on high for 11/2 hours.

3 About 20 minutes before the end of the cooking time, arrange the salmon in a single layer in a shallow dish. Combine the remaining cumin, the chilli powder, turmeric, vinegar and salt in a bowl to make a paste, then rub over the salmon and leave at room temperature while the sauce finishes cooking.

4 Add the salmon to the sauce, arranging them in a single layer and spoon some of the sauce over the top. Cover, reduce the temperature to low and cook for 45 minutes–1 hour, or until the salmon is opaque and tender.

5 Transfer the fish to a serving dish, spoon over the sauce and garnish with coriander. Serve with the rice.

Nutritional information per portion: Energy 363Kcal/1512kJ; Protein 35.9g; Carbohydrate 5.1g, of which sugars 4.2g; Fat 22.2g, of which saturates 3.8g; Cholesterol 88mg; Calcium 59mg; Fibre 0.5g; Sodium 275mg.

Red mullet braised on a bed of fennel

These pretty pink fish have a wonderful firm flesh and sweet flavour. They are usually cooked whole, but you can remove the heads if there is not enough room. Other small whole fish, such as sardines, or fish fillets, such as salmon, cod and hake, can also be cooked in this way.

SERVES 4

10ml/2 tsp fennel seeds
5ml/1 tsp chopped fresh thyme
30ml/2 tbsp chopped fresh parsley
1 garlic clove, crushed
10ml/2 tsp olive oil
4 red mullet, about 225g/8oz each,
    cleaned, scaled and fins trimmed
lemon wedges, to serve

FOR THE FENNEL

8 ripe tomatoes
2 fennel bulbs
30ml/2 tbsp olive oil
120ml/4fl oz/$^1/_2$ cup boiling fish
    or vegetable stock
10ml/2 tsp balsamic vinegar
salt and ground black pepper

1 Crush the fennel seeds using a mortar and pestle, then work in the chopped thyme and parsley, garlic and olive oil.

2 Use a sharp knife to make deep slashes on each side of the fish. Push the paste into the cuts and spread any excess inside the body cavities. Place the fish on a plate, loosely cover with clear film (plastic wrap) and leave to marinate.

3 Meanwhile, put the tomatoes in a heatproof bowl, add boiling water to cover and leave to stand for 1 minute. Drain and cool under cold running water and peel off the skins. Quarter the tomatoes, seed and cut into small dice. Trim the feathery fronds from the fennel, then cut the bulbs into 1cm/$^1/_2$ in slices from the top to the root end.

4 Heat the olive oil in a frying pan and cook the fennel slices over a medium heat for about 10 minutes, or until just starting to colour. Transfer the fennel to the cooking pot. Add the diced tomatoes, stock, vinegar, salt and pepper, cover with the lid and cook on high for 2 hours.

5 Give the fennel sauce a stir, then place the fish on top in a single layer. Cover and cook for 1 hour, or until the fish is cooked through and tender. Serve with lemon wedges.

Nutritional information per portion: Energy 194Kcal/816kJ; Protein 26.5g; Carbohydrate 4.2g, of which sugars 4.1g; Fat 8.1g, of which saturates 1.2g; Cholesterol 63mg; Calcium 95mg; Fibre 3.0g; Sodium 239mg.

Skate with tomato and Pernod sauce

The classic way of serving skate is with a browned butter sauce, but here it is given a Mediterranean twist with tomatoes, olives, orange and Pernod. If time allows, soak the fish in salted water for a few hours to firm up the flesh.

SERVES 4

15ml/1 tbsp olive oil
1 small onion, finely chopped
2 fresh thyme sprigs
grated rind of 1/2 orange
15ml/1 tbsp Pernod
400g/14oz can chopped tomatoes
50g/2oz/1 cup stuffed green olives

1.5ml/1/4 tsp caster (superfine)
   sugar
4 small skate wings
plain (all-purpose) flour, for coating
salt and ground black pepper
15ml/1 tbsp basil leaves, to garnish
lime wedges, to serve

1 Heat the oil in a pan, add the onion and fry gently for 10 minutes. Stir in the thyme and orange rind and cook for 1 minute. Add the Pernod, tomatoes, olives, sugar and a little salt and pepper, and heat until just below boiling point. Tip the mixture into the cooking pot and switch on to high. Cover with the lid and cook for 1 1/2 hours.

2 Meanwhile, rinse the skate wings under cold water and pat dry on kitchen paper.

3 Sprinkle the flour on a large, flat dish and season well with salt and ground black pepper. Coat each skate wing in the flour, shaking off any excess, then place on top of the tomato sauce. Re-cover the cooking pot and reduce the temperature to low. Cook for 1 1/2–2 hours, or until the skate is cooked and flakes easily.

4 Place the fish on to warmed serving plates and spoon over the tomato and Pernod sauce. Sprinkle over the basil leaves and serve with a wedge of lime for squeezing over.

Nutritional information per portion: Energy 144Kcal/606kJ; Protein 15.5g; Carbohydrate 8.1g, of which sugars 3.7g; Fat 4.8g, of which saturates 0.7g; Cholesterol 35mg; Calcium 37mg; Fibre 1.4g; Sodium 366mg.

Basque-style tuna

In Spain, this traditional fisherman's stew is known as marmitako. *It used to be cooked at sea on the fishing boats, and takes its name from the cooking pot, known in France as a* marmite.

SERVES 4

30ml/2 tbsp olive oil

1 onion, finely chopped

1 garlic clove, finely chopped

75ml/2¹/₂fl oz/¹/₃ cup white wine, preferably Spanish

150ml/¹/₄ pint/²/₃ cup boiling stock

200g/7oz can chopped tomatoes

5ml/1 tsp paprika

2.5ml/¹/₂ tsp dried crushed chillies

450g/1lb waxy new potatoes, cut into 1cm/¹/₂in chunks

1 red and 1 yellow (bell) pepper, chopped

1 small sprig of fresh rosemary

1 bay leaf

450g/1lb fresh tuna, cut into 2.5cm/ 1in chunks

salt and ground black pepper

crusty bread, to serve

1 Heat the oil in a large frying pan, add the onion and fry gently for 10 minutes until soft and translucent. Stir in the garlic, followed by the wine, stock, tomatoes, paprika and chillies. Bring to just below boiling point, then carefully pour the mixture into the cooking pot.

2 Add the chunks of potato, red and yellow pepper, sprig of rosemary and the bay leaf to the pot and stir to combine. Cover the slow cooker with the lid and cook on high for 2–2¹/₂ hours, or until the potatoes are just tender, then season the sauce to taste with salt and a little ground black pepper.

3 Stir the chunks of tuna into the sauce. Cover the slow cooker and cook for 15–20 minutes, or until the fish is firm and opaque.

4 Remove the rosemary and bay leaf, then ladle the stew into warmed dishes, grind over a little more black pepper and serve with crusty bread.

Nutritional information per portion: Energy 297Kcal/1256kJ; Protein 30.1g; Carbohydrate 27.5g, of which sugars 9.6g; Fat 6.g, of which saturates 1.2g; Cholesterol 57mg; Calcium 39mg; Fibre 3.2g; Sodium 397mg.

West coast fisherman's stew

Many of the little ports on the west coast of Scotland still land a small catch and often there will be a box of bits and pieces, perhaps a monkfish or some small haddock, a few prawns and small crabs. Therein lies a feast waiting to be made.

SERVES 4

30ml/2 tbsp olive oil
1 large onion, roughly chopped
1 leek, roughly chopped
2 garlic cloves, crushed
450g/1lb ripe tomatoes, roughly chopped
5ml/1 tsp tomato purée (paste)
a piece of pared orange peel
a few parsley stalks and fennel fronds
1 bay leaf
250ml/8fl oz/1 cup dry white wine
1kg/2¼lb mixed fish fillets, such as
    salmon, monkfish and haddock, cut
    into chunks, and prepared shellfish
 200ml/7fl oz/scant 1 cup boiling water
salt and ground black pepper
chopped fresh parsley, to garnish

1 Heat the olive oil in a large pan, then sweat the onion and leek until soft. Add the garlic, tomatoes and tomato purée, and cook for 5 minutes.

2 Add the orange peel, herbs and wine, and add a little salt and ground black pepper. Bring to the

boil then transfer to the cooking pot. Switch the slow cooker to low. Stir in the fish and add enough boiling water to just cover. Cover and cook for 4–5 hours.

3 Transfer the stew to warmed soup plates and serve garnished with chopped fresh parsley.

Nutritional information per portion: Energy 341kcal/1432kJ; Protein 47.5g; Carbohydrate 6.5g, of which sugars 5.8g; Fat 7.8g, of which saturates 1.2g; Cholesterol 115mg; Calcium 53mg; Fibre 2.3g; Sodium 165mg.

Haddock with spicy Puy lentils

Dark brown Puy lentils have a delicate taste and texture and hold their shape during cooking, which makes them particularly good for slow cooker dishes.

SERVES 4

175g/6oz/³⁄₄ cup Puy lentils
600ml/1 pint/2¹⁄₂ cups near-boiling
   vegetable stock
30ml/2 tbsp olive oil
1 onion, finely chopped
2 celery sticks, finely chopped
1 red chilli, halved, seeded and finely
   chopped
2.5ml/¹⁄₂ tsp ground cumin
four thick 150g/5oz pieces of haddock
   fillet or steak
10ml/2 tsp lemon juice
25g/1oz/2 tbsp butter, softened
5ml/1 tsp finely grated lemon rind
salt and ground black pepper
lemon wedges, to garnish

1 Put the lentils in a sieve (strainer) and rinse under cold running water. Drain well, then tip into the cooking pot. Pour over the hot vegetable stock, cover with the lid and switch the slow cooker on to high.

2 Heat the oil in a frying pan, add the onion and cook gently for 8 minutes. Stir in the celery, chilli and cumin, and cook for a further 2 minutes, or until soft but not coloured. Add the mixture to the lentils, stir, re-cover and cook for about 2¹⁄₂ hours.

3 Meanwhile, rinse the haddock pieces and pat dry on kitchen paper. Sprinkle them with the lemon juice. In a clean bowl, beat together the butter, lemon rind, salt and a generous amount of ground black pepper.

4 Put the haddock on top of the lentils, then dot the lemon butter over the top of the fish. Cover and cook for 45 minutes–1 hour, or until the fish flakes easily, the lentils are tender and most of the stock has been absorbed. Transfer the lentils and haddock to warmed serving plates and serve immediately, garnished with the lemon wedges.

Nutritional information per portion: Energy 366Kcal/1538kJ; Protein 38.9g; Carbohydrate 25.2g, of which sugars 3.2g; Fat 12.8g, of which saturates 4.3g; Cholesterol 82mg; Calcium 64mg; Fibre 4.7g; Sodium 353mg.

Swordfish in barbecue sauce

This is an ideal way to cook any firm fish steaks. The warmly spiced smoky sauce goes particularly well with meaty fish, such as swordfish, shark and tuna. Choose smaller, thicker fish steaks rather than large, thinner ones, so that they will fit in the slow cooker.

SERVES 4

15ml/1 tbsp sunflower oil
1 small onion, very finely chopped
1 garlic clove, crushed
2.5ml/½ tsp chilli powder
15ml/1 tbsp Worcestershire sauce
15ml/1 tbsp soft light brown sugar
15ml/1 tbsp balsamic vinegar
15ml/1 tbsp American mustard
150ml/¼ pint/⅔ cup tomato juice
4 swordfish steaks, about 115g/4oz each
salt and ground black pepper
fresh flat-leaf parsley, to garnish
boiled or steamed rice, to serve

1 Heat the oil in a frying pan, add the onion and cook gently for 10 minutes, until soft. Stir in the garlic and chilli powder and cook for a few seconds, then add the Worcestershire sauce, sugar, balsamic vinegar, mustard and tomato juice. Heat gently, stirring, until nearly boiling.

2 Pour half the sauce into the cooking pot. Rinse the fish, pat dry on kitchen paper and arrange in a single layer on top of the sauce. Top with the remaining sauce.

3 Cover the slow cooker with a lid and switch on to high. Cook for 2–3 hours, or until the fish is tender.

4 Carefully transfer the fish to warmed serving plates and spoon the barbecue sauce over the top. Garnish with sprigs of flat-leaf parsley and serve immediately with boiled or steamed rice.

Nutritional information per portion: Energy 158Kcal/670kJ; Protein 27.3g; Carbohydrate 4.9g, of which sugars 4.5g; Fat 3.5g, of which saturates 0.6g; Cholesterol 59mg; Calcium 21mg; Fibre 0.2g; Sodium 414mg.

Northern Thai fish curry

Thin, soupy, strongly flavoured curries are typical of the northern region of Thailand. Fragrant lemon grass, zesty galangal and salty Thai fish sauce come together to give this dish its characteristic Thai flavour. Serve with lots of sticky rice to soak up the juices.

SERVES 4

450g/1lb salmon fillet
475ml/16fl oz/2 cups near-boiling
   vegetable stock
4 shallots, very finely chopped
1 garlic clove, crushed
2.5cm/1in piece fresh galangal or ginger,
   finely chopped

1 lemon grass stalk, finely chopped
2.5ml/$^1/_2$ tsp dried chilli flakes
15ml/1 tbsp Thai fish sauce
5ml/1 tsp palm sugar or light
   muscovado (brown) sugar

1 Wrap the salmon fillet in clear film (plastic wrap) and place in the freezer for 30–40 minutes to firm up slightly.

2 Unwrap the fish, and carefully remove and discard the skin. Using a sharp knife, cut the fish into 2.5cm/1in cubes and remove any stray bones with your fingers or a pair of tweezers.

3 Place the cubed fish in a bowl, cover with clear film (plastic wrap) and leave to stand at room temperature.

4 Meanwhile, pour the hot vegetable stock into the ceramic cooking pot and switch the slow cooker to high.

5 Add the shallots, garlic, galangal or ginger, lemon grass, chilli flakes, fish sauce and sugar to the pot and stir to combine. Cover with the lid and cook for 2 hours.

6 Add the cubes of salmon to the stock and cook for 15 minutes. Turn off the slow cooker and leave to stand for a further 10–15 minutes, or until the fish is cooked through. Serve immediately.

Nutritional information per portion: Energy 216Kcal/902kJ; Protein 23.2g; Carbohydrate 2.7g, of which sugars 2.2g; Fat 12.6g, of which saturates 2.1g; Cholesterol 56mg; Calcium 30mg; Fibre 0.2g; Sodium 522mg.

Poultry and meat

The slow cooker is perfect for making all manner of stews, pot roasts, casseroles, braised dishes and curries. This chapter is packed with fantastic recipe ideas using poultry, game and meat as the basis of the dish. The versatility of the slow cooker means there is something here for everyone.

Chicken fricassée

This fricassée dish has a wonderfully rich sauce of cream and fresh herbs. It is perfect for entertaining because you can prepare it in advance, then leave it to simmer while you enjoy the company of your guests.

SERVES 4

25g/1oz/2 tbsp butter
30ml/2 tbsp sunflower oil
1.2–1.3kg/2¹/₂–3lb chicken, cut into
   pieces, rinsed
45ml/3 tbsp plain (all-purpose) flour
250ml/8fl oz/1 cup dry white wine
600ml/1 pint/2¹/₂ cups boiling
   chicken stock
1 bouquet garni
5ml/1 tsp lemon juice

225g/8oz/3 cups button (white)
   mushrooms, trimmed
20 small even-size button (pearl) onions
   or shallots, peeled
75ml/2¹/₂fl oz/¹/₃ cup double
   (heavy) cream
45ml/3 tbsp chopped fresh parsley
salt and ground black pepper
mashed potatoes and steamed seasonal
   vegetables, to serve

1 Melt half the butter with the oil in a large frying pan. Add the chicken and cook until browned. Using a slotted spoon, transfer the chicken to the cooking pot.

2 Stir the flour into the pan juices, then blend in the wine. Stir in the stock and add the bouquet garni and the lemon juice. Bring to the boil, stirring, until thick. Season and pour over the chicken. Cover and switch the cooker to high.

3 Clean the frying pan, then add the remaining butter and heat gently until melted. Add the mushrooms and onions or shallots and cook for 5 minutes until browned. Tip into the cooking pot. Re-cover the slow cooker and cook on high for 3–4 hours, or until the chicken is cooked and tender.

4 Using a slotted spoon, remove the chicken and vegetables to a warmed serving dish. Add the cream and 30ml/2 tbsp of the parsley to the sauce and whisk to combine. Check the seasoning and adjust if necessary, then pour the sauce over the chicken and vegetables. Sprinkle with the remaining parsley and serve with mashed potatoes and seasonal vegetables.

Nutritional information per portion: Energy 613Kcal/2563kJ; Protein 53.1g; Carbohydrate 36.4g, of which sugars 17.9g; Fat 25g, of which saturates 11.1g; Cholesterol 196mg; Calcium 128mg; Fibre 5.3g; Sodium 396mg.

Layered chicken and mushroom bake

This rich, creamy dish makes a hearty winter supper. The thick sauce combines with juices from the mushrooms and chicken during cooking to make a well-flavoured gravy.

SERVES 4

15ml/1 tbsp olive oil

4 large chicken breast portions, cut into chunks

40g/1¹/₂oz/3 tbsp butter

1 leek, finely sliced into rings

25g/1oz/¹/₄ cup plain (all-purpose) flour

550ml/18fl oz/2¹/₂ cups milk

5ml/1 tsp Worcestershire sauce (optional)

5ml/1 tsp wholegrain mustard

1 carrot, finely diced

225g/8oz/3 cups button (white) mushrooms, thinly sliced

900g/2lb potatoes, thinly sliced

salt and ground black pepper

1 Heat the oil in a large pan. Add the chicken and fry until beginning to brown. Remove the chicken using a slotted spoon. Add 25g/1oz/2 tbsp of the butter to the pan and heat until melted. Stir in the leek and fry gently for 10 minutes. Sprinkle the flour over, then turn off the heat and gradually stir in the milk until smooth. Slowly bring to the boil, stirring, until thickened.

2 Remove from the heat and stir in the Worcestershire sauce, if using, mustard, carrot, mushrooms and chicken. Season generously.

3 Arrange enough potato slices to cover the base of the ceramic cooking pot. Spoon one-third of the chicken mixture over the top, then cover with a layer of potatoes. Repeat layering, finishing with a layer of potatoes. Dot the remaining butter on top.

4 Cover and cook on high for 4 hours, or until the potatoes are cooked and tender when pierced with a skewer. If you like, place the dish under a moderate grill (broiler) for 5 minutes to brown lightly, then serve immediately.

Nutritional information per portion: Energy 461Kcal/1943kJ; Protein 42.4g; Carbohydrate 43.8g, of which sugars 5.2g; Fat 14.1g, of which saturates 6.4g; Cholesterol 126.3mg; Calcium 49mg; Fibre 4.3g; Sodium 351mg.

Apricot and almond stuffed chicken

Couscous makes a delicious base for this sweet-and-sour stuffing flavoured with apricots and almonds. The orange marmalade adds tanginess to the sauce, as well as thickening it slightly.

SERVES 4

50g/2oz/¼ cup dried apricots
150ml/¼ pint/²⁄₃ cup orange juice
4 skinned boneless chicken breast
    portions
50g/2oz/¹⁄₃ cup instant couscous
150ml/¼ pint/²⁄₃ cup boiling
    chicken stock
25g/1oz/¼ cup chopped toasted
    almonds
1.5ml/¼ tsp dried tarragon
1 egg yolk
30ml/2 tbsp orange jelly marmalade
salt and ground black pepper
boiled or steamed basmati and wild rice,
    to serve

1 Soak the apricots in the orange juice in a bowl. Cut a deep pocket horizontally in each chicken breast. Put the chicken between two sheets of oiled baking parchment, then beat with a rolling pin until thinner.

2 Put the couscous in a bowl and spoon over 50ml/2fl oz/¼ cup of the stock. Leave to stand for 2–3 minutes, or until the stock has been absorbed.

3 Drain the apricots, reserving the juice, then stir them into the couscous with the almonds and tarragon. Season, then stir in enough egg yolk to bind them together. Divide the stuffing between the chickens, then secure with cocktail sticks (toothpicks). Place the chicken in the cooking pot.

4 Stir the marmalade into the remaining stock until dissolved, then stir in the orange juice. Season and pour over the chicken. Cover and cook on high for 3–5 hours, or until cooked. Remove the chicken. Tip the sauce into a pan and boil until reduced by half. Serve the chicken with the sauce and rice.

Nutritional information per portion: Energy 379Kcal/1604kJ; Protein 40.2g; Carbohydrate 38g, of which sugars 27g; Fat 8.5g, of which saturates 1.3g; Cholesterol 155mg; Calcium 61mg; Fibre 1.6g; Sodium 117mg.

Hen in a pot with parsley sauce

Although harder to find nowadays, a boiling fowl will feed a family well. A large chicken could replace the boiling fowl. Serve with potatoes boiled in their jackets and cabbage.

SERVES 6

1.6–1.8kg/3¹/₂–4lb boiling fowl or
   whole chicken
¹/₂ lemon, sliced
small bunch of fresh flat-leaf parsley
   and thyme
675g/1¹/₂lb carrots, cut into
   large chunks
12 shallots or small onions, left whole
salt and ground black pepper

FOR THE SAUCE

50g/2oz/¹/₂ cup butter
50g/2oz/¹/₂ cup plain (all-purpose)
   flour
15ml/1 tbsp lemon juice
60ml/4 tbsp chopped flat-leaf parsley
150ml/¹/₂ pint/²/₃ cup milk
salt and ground black pepper
sprigs of flat-leaf parsley, to garnish

1 Rinse the boiling fowl or chicken under cold water and place in the cooking pot. Add the lemon, parsley and thyme, carrots and onions and season well.

2 Pour in near-boiling water to just cover the fowl and vegetables. Cover, switch the slow cooker to high and cook for 1 hour. Skim off any scum and fat using a slotted spoon. Re-cover and cook for 2–2¹/₂ hours, or until the fowl is cooked and tender. Using a slotted spoon, lift the fowl on to a warmed serving dish, arrange the vegetables around it and keep warm.

3 Strain the cooking liquid into a pan and boil uncovered to reduce by a third. Strain and leave to settle for 2 minutes, then skim the fat off the surface.

4 Melt the butter in a pan, add the flour and cook, stirring, for 1 minute. Gradually stir in the stock and bring to the boil. Add the lemon juice, parsley and milk to the pan. Season and simmer for another 1–2 minutes.

5 To serve, pour a little of the sauce over the fowl and add the carrots and onions, then garnish with a few sprigs of fresh parsley, and take to the table for carving. Pour the rest of the sauce into a sauceboat and serve separately.

Nutritional information per portion: Energy 509Kcal/2114kJ; Protein 36.2g; Carbohydrate 20.1g, of which sugars 12.2g; Fat 32g, of which saturates 11.4g; Cholesterol 195mg; Calcium 109mg; Fibre 4g; Sodium 214mg.

Chicken with chipotle sauce

Spicy-hot and deliciously rich and smoky, this dish of chicken cooked in a rich chilli sauce is great served with rice for a tasty, healthy supper. The purée can be prepared ahead of time if you like.

SERVES 6

6 chipotle chillies
200ml/7fl oz/scant 1 cup boiling water
200ml/7fl oz/scant 1 cup chicken stock
45ml/3 tbsp vegetable oil
3 onions, halved and sliced
6 boneless chicken breast portions,
   skinned and trimmed of fat
salt and ground black pepper
fresh oregano, to garnish

1 Put the chillies in a bowl and cover with the boiling water. Leave to stand for 30 minutes until very soft. Drain, reserving the soaking water. Cut off the stalk from each chilli, then slit the chilli lengthways and scrape out the seeds.

2 Chop the chillies roughly and put in a food processor or blender. Add enough chicken stock to the soaking water to make it up to 400ml/14fl oz/1²/₃ cups, then pour into the food processor or blender. Process until smooth.

3 Heat the oil in a frying pan. Add the onions and cook, stirring, over a medium heat for 5 minutes, or until soft but not coloured. Transfer the onions to the cooking pot and switch to high. Season.

4 Arrange the chicken in a single layer on top of the onions. Season with salt and pepper. Pour the chilli purée over the chicken. Cover and cook for 3–4 hours, or until the chicken is cooked through. Garnish with fresh oregano and serve.

Nutritional information per portion: Energy 235Kcal/989kJ; Protein 36.9g; Carbohydrate 5.9g, of which sugars 4.2g; Fat 7.3g, of which saturates 1.1g; Cholesterol 105mg; Calcium 26mg; Fibre 1.1g; Sodium 92mg.

Drunken chicken

Flavoured with a mixture of sherry and tequila, this rich casserole makes a great meal for any occasion. Serve with bowls of steamed or plain boiled rice or with warmed flour tortillas.

SERVES 4

150g/5oz/1 cup raisins
120ml/4fl oz/¹/₂ cup sherry
115g/4oz/1 cup plain (all-purpose) flour
2.5ml/¹/₂ tsp salt
2.5ml/¹/₂ tsp ground black pepper
45ml/3 tbsp vegetable oil
8 skinless chicken thighs
1 onion, halved and thinly sliced
2 garlic cloves, crushed
2 tart eating apples, diced
115g/4oz/1 cup flaked (sliced) almonds
1 slightly under-ripe plantain, peeled
    and sliced
300ml/¹/₂ pint/1¹/₄ cups boiling
    chicken stock
120ml/4fl oz/¹/₂ cup tequila
chopped fresh herbs, to garnish

1 Put the raisins in a small bowl and add the sherry. Set aside to soak.

2 Meanwhile, combine the flour, salt and pepper and spread the mixture out on a large plate. Heat 30ml/2 tbsp of the oil in a large frying pan. Coat each chicken thigh in the flour, then fry, turning frequently, until browned all over. Drain well on kitchen paper.

3 Heat the remaining oil in the pan, add the onion and fry for 5 minutes, or until soft and beginning to brown. Stir in the garlic, then remove the pan from the heat. Tip the onions and garlic into the cooking pot and switch the slow cooker to high.

4 Add the apples to the pot, then sprinkle with the almonds, plantain and raisins. Pour in the sherry, stock and tequila and stir. Add the chicken to the mixture, pressing them down into the stock so that they are covered. Cover and cook for 3 hours until the chicken is tender. Sprinkle with herbs to serve.

Nutritional information per portion: Energy 529Kcal/2227kJ; Protein 23.1g; Carbohydrate 63.7g, of which sugars 34.1g; Fat 11.5g, of which saturates 1.8g; Cholesterol 94.5mg; Calcium 76mg; Fibre 2.9g; Sodium 401mg.

Spring chicken braised in bacon sauce

Sweet, succulent and tangy with the flavour of apples and thyme, this delicious stew makes a great alternative to the classic roast. Baby spring chickens can weigh 350–500g/12oz–1¼lb. Be sure to buy large ones because the smaller birds are only big enough for a single serving.

SERVES 4

2 large spring chickens
25g/1oz/2 tbsp unsalted (sweet) butter
10ml/2 tsp sunflower oil
115g/4oz chopped bacon pieces or
   smoked streaky (fatty) bacon
2 leeks, sliced
175g/6oz/2¼ cup small button (white)
   mushrooms, trimmed
120ml/4fl oz/½ cup apple juice, plus a
   further 15ml/1 tbsp

120ml/4fl oz/½ cup chicken stock
30ml/2 tbsp clear honey
10ml/2 tsp chopped fresh thyme or
   2.5ml/½ tsp dried
225g/8oz crisp red dessert apples,
   thickly sliced
10ml/2 tsp cornflour (cornstarch)
salt and ground black pepper
creamy mashed potatoes and pan-fried or
   steamed baby leeks, to serve

1 Carefully split the spring chickens in half to make four portions. Rinse the portions well under cold running water, then pat dry using kitchen paper. Heat the butter and oil in a large pan and add the spring chickens. Fry, turning the pieces over, until lightly browned on all sides. Transfer the chickens to the cooking pot, leaving the cooking fat in the pan.

2 Add the chopped bacon to the pan and cook for about 5 minutes, stirring occasionally, until beginning to brown. Using a slotted spoon transfer the bacon to the cooking pot, leaving all the fat and juices behind.

3 Add the leeks and mushrooms to the pan and cook for a few minutes until they begin to soften and the mushrooms begin to release their juices. Pour 120ml/4fl oz/½ cup apple juice and the stock into the pan, then stir in the honey and thyme. Season. Bring the mixture almost to boiling point, then pour over the chicken and bacon. Cover, switch the cooker to high and cook for 2 hours.

4 Add the apples to the cooking pot, submerging them in the liquid to stop them turning brown. Cook for 2 hours, or until the chicken and vegetables are cooked and tender. Remove the chicken and keep warm. Blend the cornflour with 15ml/1 tbsp apple juice and stir into the cooking liquid until thickened. Taste and adjust the seasoning, if necessary. Serve with mashed potatoes and pan-fried or steamed baby leeks.

Nutritional information per portion: Energy 465Kcal/1945kJ; Protein 32.8g; Carbohydrate 25.9g, of which sugars 20.7g; Fat 26.3g, of which saturates 9.5g; Cholesterol 172mg; Calcium 40mg; Fibre 3.3g; Sodium 632mg.

Dorowat

The long-simmered stews eaten in Ethiopia are served with a pancake-like flatbread called injera. *Hard-boiled eggs are added towards the end of cooking to soak up the flavour of the spices.*

SERVES 4

30ml/2 tbsp vegetable oil
2 large onions, chopped
3 garlic cloves, chopped
2.5cm/1in piece peeled and finely
   chopped fresh root ginger
175ml/6fl oz/³⁄₄ cup chicken or
   vegetable stock
250ml/8fl oz/1 cup passata (bottled
   strained tomatoes) or 400g/14oz can
   chopped tomatoes
seeds from 5 cardamom pods
2.5ml/¹⁄₂ tsp ground turmeric
large pinch of ground cinnamon
large pinch of ground cloves
large pinch of grated nutmeg
1.3kg/3lb chicken, cut into 8–12 portions
4 hard-boiled eggs
cayenne pepper or hot paprika, to taste
salt and ground black pepper
roughly chopped fresh coriander
   (cilantro) and onion rings, to garnish
flatbread or rice, to serve

1 Heat the oil in a large pan, add the onions and cook for 10 minutes until softened. Add the garlic and ginger and cook for 1–2 minutes. Add the stock and the passata to the pan. Bring to the boil and cook, stirring frequently, for about 10 minutes, or until the mixture has thickened, then season.

2 Transfer the mixture to the ceramic cooking pot and stir in the cardamom, turmeric, cinnamon, cloves and nutmeg. Add the chicken in a single layer, pushing the pieces down into the sauce.

3 Cover and cook on high for 3 hours. Remove the shells from the eggs, then prick the eggs a few times with a fork or very fine skewer. Add to the sauce and cook for 30–45 minutes, or until the chicken is cooked through and tender. Season to taste with cayenne pepper or hot paprika. Garnish with coriander and onion rings and serve with flatbread or rice.

Nutritional information per portion: Energy 388Kcal/1629kJ; Protein 54.6g; Carbohydrate 13g, of which sugars 9.6g; Fat 13.4g, of which saturates 2.8g; Cholesterol 13mg; Calcium 81mg; Fibre 2.5g; Sodium 311mg.

Jamaican jerk chicken

The word "jerk" refers to the herb and spice seasoning traditionally used to marinate meat in Jamaica. It was originally used only for pork, but jerked chicken is just as good.

SERVES 4

8 chicken pieces, such as thighs and legs
15ml/1 tbsp sunflower oil
15g/½ oz/1 tbsp unsalted (sweet) butter

FOR THE SAUCE

1 bunch of spring onions (scallions), trimmed and finely chopped
2 garlic cloves, crushed
1 hot red chilli pepper, halved, seeded and finely chopped
5ml/1 tsp ground allspice
2.5ml/½ tsp ground cinnamon
5ml/1 tsp dried thyme
1.5ml/¼ tsp freshly grated nutmeg
10ml/2 tsp demerara (raw) sugar
15ml/1 tbsp plain (all-purpose) flour
300ml/½ pint/1¼ cups chicken stock
15ml/1 tbsp red or white wine vinegar
15ml/1 tbsp lime juice
10ml/2 tsp tomato purée (paste)
salt and ground black pepper
salad leaves or rice, to serve

1 Wipe the chicken pieces, then pat dry on kitchen paper. Heat the oil and butter in a frying pan until melted, then add the chicken, in batches, and cook until browned on all sides. Remove with a slotted spoon and transfer to the cooking pot. Switch the slow cooker to high.

2 Add the spring onions, garlic and chilli to the frying pan and cook gently for 4–5 minutes, or until softened. Stir in the allspice, cinnamon, thyme, nutmeg and sugar. Sprinkle in the flour and stir to mix, then gradually add the stock, stirring until the mixture bubbles and thickens. Remove from the heat.

3 Stir the vinegar, lime juice, tomato purée and some seasoning into the sauce. Pour over the chicken, cover and cook on high for 3–4 hours, or until the chicken is cooked and very tender. Remove the chicken from the sauce and place on a serving dish. Serve with salad leaves or rice.

Nutritional information per portion: Energy 189Kcal/794kJ; Protein 21g; Carbohydrate 7g, of which sugars 3.1g; Fat 8.8g, of which saturates 3.1g; Cholesterol 107mg; Calcium 24mg; Fibre 0.5g; Sodium 238mg.

Spicy chicken jambalaya

This classic Creole dish is great for a family supper, served with a simple salad. Spicy red Spanish chorizo sausage gives the stew a real flavour boost.

SERVES 6

225g/8oz skinless, boneless chicken
   breast portions
175g/6oz piece raw smoked gammon
   or bacon
30ml/2 tbsp olive oil
1 large onion, chopped
2 garlic cloves, crushed
2 sticks celery, diced
5ml/1 tsp chopped fresh thyme or
   2.5ml/^{1}/$_2$ tsp dried thyme
5ml/1 tsp mild chilli powder
2.5ml/^{1}/$_2$ tsp ground ginger
10ml/2 tsp tomato purée (paste)
2 dashes of Tabasco sauce
750ml/1^1/$_4$ pints/3 cups boiling
   chicken stock
300g/10oz/1^1/$_2$ cups easy-cook
   (converted) rice
115g/4oz chorizo sausage (cooked), sliced
30ml/2 tbsp chopped fresh flat-leaf
   parsley, plus extra, to garnish
salt and ground black pepper

1 Cut the chicken into 2.5cm/1in cubes and season. Trim any fat off the gammon or bacon, then cut the meat into 1cm/^{1}/$_2$in cubes.

2 Heat 15ml/1 tbsp of the oil in a pan, add the onion and fry for 5 minutes, until beginning to colour. Stir in the garlic, celery, thyme, chilli powder and ginger and cook for 1 minute. Transfer to the cooking pot and turn the slow cooker to high.

3 Heat the remaining 15ml/1 tbsp oil in the pan, add the chicken and fry until lightly browned. Add the chicken to the cooking pot with the gammon. Add the tomato purée and Tabasco to the stock and whisk together. Pour into the cooker, cover and cook on high for 1^1/$_2$ hours.

4 Sprinkle the rice into the cooking pot and stir to mix well. Cover and cook on high for 45 minutes–1 hour, or until the rice is almost tender and most of the stock has been absorbed. Check towards the end of cooking time and add a little extra stock if it is dry. Stir in the chorizo and cook on high for a further 15 minutes, or until heated through. Stir in the parsley and check the seasoning.

5 Turn off the slow cooker and leave the jambalaya to stand for 10 minutes. Fluff the rice with a fork, then serve with chopped parsley sprinkled on top.

Nutritional information per portion: Energy 384Kcal/1617kJ; Protein 21.2g; Carbohydrate 48.6g, of which sugars 2.9g; Fat 13g, of which saturates 3.6g; Cholesterol 43mg; Calcium 57mg; Fibre 1.1g; Sodium 630mg.

Caribbean peanut chicken

Peanut butter adds a delicious richness and depth of flavour to this spicy rice dish. It is a classic ingredient used in many slow-cooked Caribbean curries and stews.

SERVES 4

45ml/3 tbsp groundnut (peanut) or
    sunflower oil

1 garlic clove, crushed

5ml/1 tsp chopped fresh thyme

15ml/1 tbsp curry powder

juice of half a lemon

4 skinless, boneless chicken breast
    portions, cut into thin strips

1 onion, finely chopped

2 tomatoes, peeled, seeded and chopped

1 fresh green chilli, seeded and sliced

60ml/4 tbsp smooth peanut butter

750ml/1¼ pints/3 cups boiling
    chicken stock

300g/10oz/1½ cups easy-cook
    (converted) white rice

salt and ground black pepper

lemon or lime wedges and sprigs of fresh
    flat-leaf parsley, to garnish

1 Combine 15ml/1 tbsp of the oil, garlic, thyme, curry powder and lemon juice. Add the chicken, stir and leave to stand for 1½–2 hours.

2 Meanwhile, heat the remaining oil in a pan, add the onion and fry for 10 minutes until soft. Transfer to the pot and switch the cooker to high. Add the tomatoes and chilli and stir.

3 Put the peanut butter into a bowl, then gradually blend in the stock. Pour into the pot, season and stir. Cover and cook for 1 hour.

4 Add the chicken and the marinade to the cooking pot and stir to mix thoroughly. Re-cover and cook for a further 1 hour.

5 Sprinkle the rice over the casserole, then stir to mix well. Cover and cook for a final 45 minutes–1 hour, or until the chicken and rice are cooked and the chicken is very tender.

6 Serve immediately, garnished with lemon wedges for squeezing over, and fresh parsley sprigs.

Nutritional information per portion: Energy 635Kcal/2677kJ; Protein 45.8g; Carbohydrate 70.7g, of which sugars 4.4g; Fat 20.8g, of which saturates 4.1g; Cholesterol 105mg; Calcium 65mg; Fibre 2.1g; Sodium 354mg.

Pigeons in stout

The edible meat on pigeons is mainly on the breast. The flesh is dark and, like most small birds, dry, so casseroling them in stout is an ideal cooking method.

SERVES 6

175g/6oz thick streaky (fatty)
    bacon, roughly chopped
2 onions, finely chopped
2 or 3 garlic cloves,
    crushed
seasoned flour, for coating
50g/2oz/¹/₄ cup butter
15ml/1 tbsp olive oil

6 pigeon breast portions
30ml/2 tbsp Irish whiskey (optional)
425ml/15fl oz/scant 2 cups chicken stock
300ml/¹/₂ pint/1¹/₄ cups stout
175g/6oz button (white) mushrooms
15–30ml/1–2 tbsp rowan jelly
boiled or steamed rice, to serve
salt and ground black pepper

1 Cook the bacon gently in a large frying pan until the fat runs out, then add the onions and crushed garlic and continue cooking until they are soft. Transfer to the ceramic cooking pot.

2 Coat the breast portions thickly with seasoned flour. Add the butter and oil to the pan, heat until the butter is foaming, then add the meat and brown well on all sides. Pour in the Irish whiskey, if using. Carefully set it alight and shake the pan until the flames go out – this improves the flavour. Transfer to the ceramic cooking pot and switch the slow cooker to high.

3 Stir the stock, stout and the mushrooms into the pan, and bring slowly to the boil. Transfer to the cooking pot. Cover and cook for 3–4 hours.

4 Stir rowan jelly to taste into the gravy and adjust the seasoning. Serve the pigeon breast portions with rice and the gravy while hot.

Nutritional information per portion: Energy 436Kcal/1817kJ; Protein 38.7g; Carbohydrate 6.7g, of which sugars 5.3g; Fat 27.2g, of which saturates 6.2g; Cholesterol 33mg; Calcium 48mg; Fibre 1.7g; Sodium 639mg.

Tarragon chicken in cider

Aromatic tarragon has a distinctive flavour that goes wonderfully with both cream and chicken. This recipe is truly effortless, yet provides an elegant dish for entertaining or a special family meal. Serve with sautéed potatoes and a green vegetable.

SERVES 4

15ml/1 tbsp sunflower oil
350g/12oz small button (pearl)
   onions
4 garlic cloves
4 boneless chicken breast portions,
   skin on
350ml/12fl oz/1½ cups dry (hard) cider
1 bay leaf
200g/7oz/scant 1 cup crème fraîche or
   sour cream
30ml/2 tbsp chopped fresh tarragon
15ml/1 tbsp chopped fresh parsley
salt and ground black pepper

1 Heat the oil in a frying pan, add the onions and cook for 10 minutes, or until lightly browned. Add the garlic and cook for a further 2–3 minutes. Using a slotted spoon, transfer the onions and garlic to the cooking pot. Place the chicken in the frying pan and cook for 3–4 minutes, turning once or twice until lightly browned on both sides. Transfer the chicken to the cooking pot.

2 Pour the cider into the pan, add the bay leaf, season and bring to the boil. Pour the cider and bay leaf over the chicken. Cover and cook on low for 4–5 hours, or until the chicken and onions are cooked. Lift out the chicken.

3 Stir the crème fraîche and the herbs into the sauce. Return the chicken breasts to the pot and cook for a further 30 minutes on high, or until piping hot. Serve the chicken with potatoes and a green vegetable.

Nutritional information per portion: Energy 520Kcal/2167kJ; Protein 36.9g; Carbohydrate 12.1g, of which sugars 9.2g; Fat 33.9g, of which saturates 12.9g; Cholesterol 184mg; Calcium 90mg; Fibre 1.5g; Sodium 138mg.

Fragrant chicken curry

Lentils are used to thicken the sauce in this mild, fragrant curry, and fresh coriander gives the dish a really distinctive, fresh taste. The generous quantities of spinach mean that you won't need an additional vegetable dish to balance the meal.

SERVES 4

75g/3oz/scant ½ cup red lentils
30ml/2 tbsp mild curry powder
10ml/2 tsp ground coriander
5ml/1 tsp cumin seeds
350ml/12fl oz/1½ cups boiling
    vegetable or chicken stock
8 chicken thighs, skinned
225g/8oz fresh spinach, shredded
15ml/1 tbsp chopped fresh
    coriander (cilantro)
salt and ground black pepper
sprigs of fresh coriander, to garnish
white or brown basmati rice and
    poppadums, to serve

1 Place the lentils in a sieve (strainer) and rinse under cold running water. Drain well, then put in the cooking pot with the curry powder, ground coriander, cumin seeds and stock. Cover and cook on high for 2 hours.

2 Add the chicken to the lentil mixture, pressing it down in a single layer. Cover and cook on high for 3 hours, or until the chicken is just tender.

3 Add the spinach to the slow cooker, carefully pressing it down into the hot liquid. Cover and cook for a further 30 minutes until wilted. Then stir in the chopped coriander.

4 Season the curry with salt and pepper to taste, then serve garnished with fresh coriander sprigs and accompanied with basmati rice and poppadums.

Nutritional information per portion: Energy 591Kcal/2490kJ; Protein 75.5g; Carbohydrate 38.2g, of which sugars 3.9g; Fat 16.1g, of which saturates 3.9g; Cholesterol 171mg; Calcium 426mg; Fibre 9.4g; Sodium 880mg.

Chicken in a cashew nut sauce

The Moguls had a profound impact on Indian cuisine, and one of their legacies is the use of nut paste, which is used here to give the curry a rich yet delicately flavoured sauce.

SERVES 4

1 large onion, roughly chopped
1 clove garlic, crushed
15ml/1 tbsp tomato purée (paste)
50g/2oz/¹⁄₂ cup cashew nuts
7.5ml/1¹⁄₂ tsp garam masala
5ml/1 tsp chilli powder
1.5ml/¹⁄₄ tsp ground turmeric
5ml/1 tsp salt
15ml/1 tbsp lemon juice
15ml/1 tbsp natural (plain) yogurt
30ml/2 tbsp vegetable oil
450g/1lb chicken breast fillets, skinned
    and cubed
175g/6oz/2¹⁄₄ cups button (white)
    mushrooms
15ml/1 tbsp sultanas (golden raisins)
300ml/¹⁄₂ pint/1¹⁄₄ cups chicken or
    vegetable stock
30ml/2 tbsp chopped fresh coriander
    (cilantro), plus extra to garnish
rice and fruit chutney, to serve

1 Put the onion, garlic, tomato purée, cashew nuts, garam masala, chilli powder, turmeric, salt, lemon juice and yogurt in a food processor and process to a paste.

2 Heat the oil in a large frying pan and fry the chicken for a few minutes, or until just beginning to brown. Using a slotted spoon, transfer the chicken to the cooking pot, leaving the oil in the pan.

3 Add the spice paste and mushrooms to the pan, lower the heat and fry gently, stirring often, for 3–4 minutes. Tip into the pot.

4 Add the sultanas to the pot and stir in the stock. Cover and switch the slow cooker to high. Cook for 3–4 hours, stirring halfway through the cooking time. The chicken should be cooked through, and the sauce fairly thick.

5 Stir the coriander into the sauce, then taste and add a little more seasoning, if necessary.

6 Serve the curry from the pot, or transfer to a serving dish, and garnish with chopped fresh coriander. Serve with rice and a fruit chutney.

Nutritional information per portion: Energy 239Kcal/1006kJ; Protein 31.6g; Carbohydrate 10.7g, of which sugars 7.6g; Fat 8.1g, of which saturates 1.7g; Cholesterol 78.9mg; Calcium 39mg; Fibre 1.9g; Sodium 696mg.

Chicken and split pea koresh

A traditional Persian koresh – a thick saucy stew served with rice – is usually made with lamb, but here chicken is used to create a lighter, lower-fat dish.

SERVES 4

50g/2oz/¼ cup green split peas
45ml/3 tbsp olive oil
1 large onion, finely chopped
450g/1lb boneless chicken thighs
350ml/12fl oz/1½ cups boiling
    chicken stock
5ml/1 tsp ground turmeric
2.5ml/½ tsp ground cinnamon
1.5ml/¼ tsp grated nutmeg
30ml/2 tbsp dried mint
2 aubergines (eggplants), diced
8 ripe tomatoes, diced
2 garlic cloves, crushed
salt and ground black pepper
fresh mint, to garnish
plain boiled rice, to serve

1 Put the split peas in a large bowl. Pour in cold water to cover and leave the split peas to soak for at least 6 hours or overnight.

2 Transfer the split peas to a sieve (strainer) and drain well. Place in a large pan, cover with cold water and bring to the boil. Boil for 10 minutes, then rinse, drain and set aside.

3 Heat 15ml/1 tbsp of the oil in a pan, add the onion and cook for 5 minutes. Add the chicken and cook until golden, then transfer to the cooking pot. Add the split peas, stock, turmeric, cinnamon, nutmeg and mint and season well. Cover and

cook on high or auto for 1 hour. Switch the slow cooker to low or leave on auto and cook for a further 3 hours, or until the chicken is just cooked and the split peas are tender.

4 Heat the remaining 30ml/2 tbsp of oil in a frying pan, add the aubergines and cook for 5 minutes until lightly browned. Add the tomatoes and garlic and cook for a further 2 minutes. Transfer the aubergine mixture to the cooking pot, stir to combine, then cook for about 1 hour.

5 Sprinkle with fresh mint leaves to garnish and serve with plain rice.

Nutritional information per portion: Energy 298Kcal/1251kJ; Protein 29.1g; Carbohydrate 18.5g, of which sugars 10.2g; Fat 12.5g, of which saturates 2.3g; Cholesterol 118mg; Calcium 48mg; Fibre 4.5g; Sodium 206mg.

Guinea fowl and spring vegetable stew

Resembling a well-flavoured chicken stew, this tasty dish of guinea fowl cooked with spring vegetables and flavoured with mustard and herbs is bound to please.

SERVES 4

1.6kg/3¹/₂lb guinea fowl
45ml/3 tbsp plain (all-purpose) flour
45ml/3 tbsp olive oil
115g/4oz pancetta, cut into tiny cubes
1 onion, chopped
3 garlic cloves, chopped
200ml/7fl oz/scant 1 cup white wine
225g/8oz baby carrots
225g/8oz baby turnips
6 baby leeks, cut into 7.5cm/3in lengths

sprig of fresh thyme
1 bay leaf
10ml/2 tsp Dijon mustard
150ml/¹/₄ pint/²/₃ cup boiling chicken or
    vegetable stock
225g/8oz shelled peas
30ml/2 tbsp chopped fresh parsley
15ml/1 tbsp chopped fresh mint
salt and ground black pepper

1 Joint the guinea fowl into eight pieces. Wipe or rinse them, then pat dry on kitchen paper. Season the flour with salt and pepper and toss the guinea fowl portions in it.

2 Heat 30ml/2 tbsp of the oil in a frying pan, add the pancetta and fry over a medium heat until lightly browned, stirring occasionally. Transfer the pancetta to the ceramic cooking pot. Add the guinea fowl portions to the pan and fry, turning, until browned on all sides. Arrange the guinea fowl in a single layer in the cooking pot on top of the pancetta.

3 Add the remaining 15ml/1 tbsp oil to the frying pan, add the onion and cook for 3–4 minutes, until just beginning to soften. Add the garlic and cook for about 1 minute, then stir in the reserved flour. Gradually stir in the wine and bring to the boil. Pour over the guinea fowl.

4 Add the carrots, turnips and leeks to the cooking pot with the thyme and bay leaf. Blend the mustard with the stock, season and pour over. Cover and cook on high for 3–4 hours, or until the meat and vegetables are tender. Add the peas and cook for a further 45 minutes. Check the seasoning, then stir in most of the herbs. Divide the stew among warmed plates, sprinkle the remaining herbs over the top and serve.

Nutritional information per portion: Energy 581Kcal/2425kJ; Protein 50.5g; Carbohydrate 29.1g, of which sugars 11.2g; Fat 26.5g, of which saturates 7.4g; Cholesterol 224mg; Calcium 109mg; Fibre 6.9g; Sodium 668mg.

Duck stew with olives

This method of cooking duck with olives, onions and wine has its roots in Provence in France. The sweetness brought out by slow-cooking the onions balances the saltiness of the olives.

SERVES 4

4 duck quarters or breast portions
225g/8oz baby (pearl) onions
2.5ml/¹/₂ tsp caster (superfine) sugar
30ml/2 tbsp plain (all-purpose) flour
250ml/8fl oz/1 cup dry red wine
250ml/8fl oz/1 cup duck or chicken stock
1 bouquet garni
115g/4oz/1 cup pitted green or black
   olives, or a combination
salt and ground black pepper

1 Put the duck skin side down in a large frying pan and cook for 10–12 minutes until browned on both sides. Place skin side up in the cooking pot. Switch the slow cooker to high.

2 Pour off most of the fat from the pan, leaving 15ml/1 tbsp behind. Add the onions and cook until beginning to colour. Sprinkle over the sugar and cook for 5 minutes until golden. Sprinkle with the flour and cook for 2 minutes.

3 Stir the wine into the onions, then the stock. Bring to the boil, then pour over the duck. Add the bouquet garni, cover and cook on high for 1 hour. Turn to low and cook for 4–5 hours.

4 Pour hot water over the olives to cover. Leave for 1 minute, then drain. Add the olives to the casserole, cover and cook for 30 minutes. Put the duck, onions and olives in a dish. Skim the fat from the cooking liquid. Season and spoon over the duck.

Nutritional information per portion: Energy 414Kcal/1736kJ; Protein 47.3g; Carbohydrate 8.2g, of which sugars 2.3g; Fat 18.5g, of which saturates 5.2g; Cholesterol 257mg; Calcium 67mg; Fibre 1.6g; Sodium 917mg.

Rabbit casserole with juniper

Because rabbit is such a lean meat, slow-cooking is an ideal way to cook it, helping to keep it moist and juicy. Using a well-flavoured marinade improves both the taste and texture of the meat.

SERVES 4

900g/2lb prepared rabbit pieces
1 onion, roughly chopped
2 garlic cloves, crushed
1 bay leaf
350ml/12fl oz/1½ cups fruity red wine
2 sprigs of fresh thyme, bruised
1 sprig of fresh rosemary, bruised
15ml/1 tbsp juniper berries, crushed
30ml/2 tbsp olive oil
15g/½oz dried porcini mushrooms
150ml/¼ pint/⅔ cup boiling water
30ml/2 tbsp chopped fresh parsley
25g/1oz/2 tbsp chilled butter, cubed
salt and ground black pepper

1 Put the rabbit in a dish with the onion, garlic, bay leaf and wine. Add the herbs and juniper berries and toss well. Marinate for at least 4 hours or overnight.

2 Remove the rabbit from the marinade, reserving the marinade, and pat dry. Heat the oil in a pan, add the meat and fry until browned. Transfer to the cooking pot. Pour the marinade into the frying pan and bring to boiling point. Pour over the rabbit, cover and switch the slow cooker to high. Cook for 1 hour.

3 Put the mushrooms in a bowl and pour over the boiling water. Soak for 1 hour, then drain, reserving the liquid. Finely chop the mushrooms.

4 Pour the mushroom liquid into the pot. Cook for 2 hours. Lift out the rabbit and strain the liquid. Return the rabbit and liquid to the pot, add the mushrooms and season. Cook for 1 hour until the meat is tender. Stir in the parsley, then put the rabbit in a dish. Whisk the butter into the sauce, one or two pieces at a time, then spoon over the rabbit.

Nutritional information per portion: Energy 356Kcal/1483kJ; Protein 32g; Carbohydrate 3.2g, of which sugars 2.3g; Fat 17.5g, of which saturates 6.3g; Cholesterol 163mg; Calcium 30mg; Fibre 0.6g; Sodium 66mg.

Pappardelle with rabbit

This rich-tasting dish comes from northern Italy, where rabbit sauces are very popular. It is ideal for entertaining as the sauce can be kept warm in the slow cooker until needed.

SERVES 4

15g/¹/₂oz dried porcini mushrooms
150ml/¹/₄ pint/²/₃ cup warm water
2 bay leaves
25g/1oz/2 tbsp butter or 15ml/1 tbsp
   olive oil
1 small onion, finely chopped
¹/₂ carrot, finely chopped
¹/₂ celery stick, finely chopped
40g/1¹/₂oz pancetta or rindless streaky
   (fatty) bacon, chopped

15ml/1 tbsp roughly chopped fresh
   flat-leaf parsley, plus extra to garnish
250g/9oz boneless rabbit meat
60ml/4 tbsp dry white wine
200g/7oz can chopped Italian plum
   tomatoes or 200ml/7fl oz/scant
   1 cup passata (bottled strained
   tomatoes)
300g/11oz fresh or dried pappardelle
salt and ground black pepper

1 Put the dried mushrooms in a bowl, pour over the water and soak for 15 minutes. Make a tear in each bay leaf, so they will release their flavour when added to the sauce.

2 Heat the butter or oil in a large frying pan until just sizzling. Add the chopped vegetables, pancetta or bacon and parsley and cook for 5 minutes.

3 Add the rabbit and fry on both sides for 3–4 minutes. Transfer to the ceramic cooking pot and switch to the high or auto setting. Add the wine and tomatoes or passata. Drain the mushrooms and strain the soaking liquid through a sieve (strainer) into the cooker. Chop the mushrooms and add to the mixture, with the bay leaves. Season, then stir well, cover with the lid and cook for 1 hour. Reduce the setting to low or leave on auto, and cook for a further 2 hours, or until the meat is tender.

4 Lift out the rabbit, cut into bitesize chunks and stir back into the sauce. Discard the bay leaves. Check the seasoning. The sauce is ready to serve, but can be kept hot in the cooker for 1–2 hours.

5 About 10 minutes before serving, cook the pasta according to the packet instructions. Drain the pasta, add to the sauce and toss well. Serve sprinkled with parsley.

Nutritional information per portion: Energy 393Kcal/1653kJ; Protein 23g; Carbohydrate 46g, of which sugars 4.9g; Fat 13.3g, of which saturates 5g; Cholesterol 46mg; Calcium 80mg; Fibre 1.1g; Sodium 128mg.

Steak and kidney pie with mustard gravy

Peppery mustard gravy flavoured with bay leaves and parsley complements the tasty chunks of beef and kidney in this classic pie. Cooking the pastry topping separately from the filling ensures it remains crisp – and is a perfect technique to use when making the pie using a slow cooker.

SERVES 4

675g/1½lb stewing steak
225g/8oz ox or lamb's kidney, trimmed
45ml/3 tbsp oil
15g/½oz/1 tbsp unsalted (sweet) butter
2 onions, chopped
30ml/2 tbsp plain (all-purpose) flour
300ml/½ pint/1¼ cups beef stock
15ml/1 tbsp tomato purée (paste)

10ml/2 tsp English mustard
2 bay leaves
375g/13oz puff pastry
beaten egg, to glaze
15ml/1 tbsp chopped fresh parsley
salt and ground black pepper
creamed potatoes and green vegetables,
    to serve

1 Cut the steak into 2.5cm/1in cubes. Cut the kidney into cubes. Heat 30ml/2 tbsp of the oil in a frying pan and brown the beef. Remove with a slotted spoon and place in the cooking pot. Switch the slow cooker on to high.

2 Add the kidney to the frying pan and brown for 1–2 minutes before adding to the beef. Add the remaining oil and the butter to the pan, add the onions and cook for 5 minutes. Stir in the flour, then remove from the heat.

3 Stir the stock into the pan, then the tomato purée and mustard. Return to the heat and bring to the boil until thickened. Pour over the meat, add the bay leaves and season. Stir and cover. Reduce the cooker to low and cook for 5–7 hours, or until the meat is tender. Discard the bay leaves.

4 Roll out the pastry and cut out a 25cm/10in round. Transfer to a baking sheet lined with baking parchment, mark the pastry into quarters, decorate and flute the edge. Cover and chill.

5 Towards the end of the cooking time, preheat the oven to 200°C/400°F/Gas 6. Brush the pastry with egg, then bake for 25 minutes. To serve, stir the parsley into the stew and spoon on to plates. Cut the pie crust into four and use to top each portion. Serve with potatoes and vegetables.

Nutritional information per portion: Energy 637Kcal/2652kJ; Protein 18.7g; Carbohydrate 46.2g, of which sugars 5.2g; Fat 43.4g, of which saturates 13.1g; Cholesterol 259mg; Calcium 99mg; Fibre 2.7g; Sodium 578mg.

Provençal beef stew

Known in France as **daube de boeuf à la Provençal,** *after the earthernware pot it was originally cooked in, this deliciously rich, fruity stew makes a perfect winter supper dish.*

SERVES 4

45ml/3 tbsp olive oil

115g/4oz lean salt pork or thick-cut bacon, diced

900g/2lb stewing steak cut into 4cm/1¹/₂in pieces

250ml/8fl oz/1 cup fruity red wine

150ml/¹/₄ pint/²/₃ cup beef stock

1 bouquet garni

1 small onion, studded with 2 cloves

1 large onion, chopped

2 carrots, sliced

2 ripe tomatoes, peeled, seeded and chopped

10ml/2 tsp tomato purée (paste)

2 garlic cloves, very finely chopped

grated rind and juice of ¹/₂ orange

15ml/1 tbsp chopped fresh parsley

salt and ground black pepper

1 Heat 15ml/1 tbsp of the oil in a frying pan, then add the pork or bacon and cook over a medium heat for 4–5 minutes, stirring, until browned and the fat is rendered.

2 Using a slotted spoon, transfer the pork or bacon to the cooking pot and switch the slow cooker to high.

3 Working in batches, add the beef to the pan in a single layer. Cook for 6–8 minutes until browned, turning to colour all sides.

4 Transfer the beef to the cooking pot and brown the rest of the meat, adding more oil when needed.

5 Pour the wine and stock over the beef in the cooking pot, then add the bouquet garni and the onion. Add the remaining oil and the onion to the frying pan and cook for a further 5 minutes. Stir in the carrots and cook for a further 5 minutes, until softened. Stir in the tomatoes, tomato purée and garlic, then transfer to the cooking pot.

6 Cover and switch the slow cooker to low. Cook for 5–7 hours, or until the beef and vegetables are very tender. Uncover and skim off any fat. Season, discard the bouquet garni and onion, and stir in the orange rind, juice and the parsley.

Nutritional information per portion: Energy 547Kcal/2286kJ; Protein 55.8g; Carbohydrate 8.7g, of which sugars 7.2g; Fat 27.8g, of which saturates 8.9g; Cholesterol 170mg; Calcium 43mg; Fibre 2g; Sodium 682mg.

Braised beef in a rich peanut sauce

Like many dishes brought to the Philippines by the Spanish, this slow-cooking Estofado, *renamed by the Filipinos as* Kari Kari, *retains much of its original charm.*

SERVES 4

45ml/3 tbsp vegetable oil
900g/2lb stewing steak, cut into
    2.5cm/1in cubes
2 onions, chopped
2 cloves garlic, crushed
5ml/1 tsp paprika
pinch of ground turmeric
225g/8oz celeriac root or swede
    (rutabaga), peeled and cut into
    2cm/¾in dice
425ml/15fl oz/1¾ cups boiling stock
15ml/1 tbsp fish or anchovy sauce
30ml/2 tbsp tamarind sauce (optional)
10ml/2 tsp soft light brown sugar
1 bay leaf
1 sprig thyme
30ml/2 tbsp smooth peanut butter
45ml/3 tbsp easy-cook (converted)
    white rice
5ml/1 tsp white wine vinegar
salt and ground black pepper

1 Heat 30ml/2 tbsp of the oil in a pan and fry the beef until browned. Transfer the meat and any juices to the cooking pot and switch the slow cooker to high.

2 Add the remaining oil to the frying pan and fry the onions gently for 10 minutes until soft. Add the garlic, paprika and turmeric and cook for a further 1 minute.

3 Transfer the mixture to the cooking pot and add the celeriac. Pour in the stock, fish sauce and taramind sauce, if using.

4 Add the sugar, bay leaf and thyme. Cover, reduce the heat to low and cook for 4 hours, or until the beef and vegetables are tender.

5 Turn the slow cooker up to high, then remove 60ml/4 tbsp of the cooking juices, transfer to a bowl and blend with the peanut butter. Stir the mixture into the casserole, sprinkle with the rice, and stir well.

6 Cover and cook for 45 minutes, or until the rice is cooked and the sauce has thickened. Stir in the vinegar and season to taste. Serve.

Nutritional information per portion: Energy 577Kcal/2408kJ; Protein 48.9g; Carbohydrate 14.1g, of which sugars 8.9g; Fat 36.8g, of which saturates 12.2g; Cholesterol 141mg; Calcium 70mg; Fibre 2.4g; Sodium 561mg.

Braised beef with horseradish

This dish makes an ideal alternative to a meat roast. The meat slowly tenderizes in the slow cooker and all the flavours blend together beautifully. It is also a great dish for entertaining because it can be prepared in advance and left to simmer on its own until you are ready to serve.

SERVES 4

30ml/2 tbsp plain (all-purpose) flour

4 x 175g/6oz braising steaks

30ml/2 tbsp sunflower oil

12 small shallots, peeled and halved

1 garlic clove, crushed

1.5ml/¼ tsp ground ginger

5ml/1 tsp curry powder

10ml/2 tsp dark muscovado (molasses) sugar

475ml/16fl oz/2 cups near-boiling beef stock

15ml/1 tbsp Worcestershire sauce

30ml/2 tbsp creamed horseradish

225g/8oz baby carrots, trimmed

1 bay leaf

salt and ground black pepper

30ml/2 tbsp chopped fresh chives, to garnish

roast vegetables, to serve

1 Place the flour in a large, flat dish and season with salt and pepper. Toss the steaks in the flour to coat. Heat the oil in a frying pan and quickly brown the steaks on both sides. Transfer them to the ceramic cooking pot.

2 Add the halved shallots to the pan and cook gently for 10 minutes, or until golden and beginning to soften. Stir in the garlic, ginger and curry powder and cook for 1 minute more, then remove from the heat.

3 Transfer the shallot mixture to the cooking pot, spreading it over the meat, and sprinkle with the sugar. Pour the beef stock over the shallots and meat, then add the Worcestershire sauce, horseradish, baby carrots and bay leaf. Stir to combine, then season. Cover and cook on high or auto for 1 hour.

4 Reduce the slow cooker to low, or leave on auto, and continue to cook the stew for a further 5–6 hours, or until the beef and vegetables are very tender.

5 Remove the bay leaf from the stew and sprinkle with the chopped chives before serving with roast vegetables.

Nutritional information per portion: Energy 478Kcal/2010kJ; Protein 62.5g; Carbohydrate 17.7g, of which sugars 9.6g; Fat 18.1g, of which saturates 7.4g; Cholesterol 176mg; Calcium 65mg; Fibre 2.5g; Sodium 423mg.

Spiced beef

This is a classic Irish dish, although it is a modern version of the traditional recipe, as it omits the initial pickling stage and takes only three or four days. Serve on brown bread, with chutney.

SERVES 6

15ml/1 tbsp coarsely ground
   black pepper
10ml/2 tsp ground ginger
15ml/1 tbsp juniper berries, crushed
15ml/1 tbsp coriander seeds,
   crushed
5ml/1 tsp ground cloves
15ml/1 tbsp ground allspice
45ml/3 tbsp soft dark brown sugar
2 bay leaves, crushed
1 small onion, finely chopped
1.8kg/4lb corned beef, silverside or
   tail end
300ml/¹/₂ pint/1¹/₄ cups Guinness
fruit chutney and brown bread, to serve

1 Blend the pepper, spices and sugar thoroughly, then mix in the bay leaves and onion. Rub the mixture into the meat, then put it into a lidded container and chill for 3–4 days, turning and rubbing with the mixture daily.

2 Put the meat into the cooking pot and barely cover with cold water. Cover with the lid and switch on to auto or high. Cook for 3 hours, then leave on auto or reduce to low and cook for a further 3–4 hours, until the meat is very tender. For the last hour add the Guinness.

3 When the joint is cooked, leave it to cool in the cooking liquid. Wrap in foil and chill until required, then slice thinly to serve. It will keep for 1 week.

COOK'S TIP
Spiced beef is excellent as finger food for parties, sliced thinly and served with sour cream lightly flavoured with horseradish and black pepper.

Nutritional information per portion: Energy 309Kcal/1301kJ; Protein 53.6g; Carbohydrate 2g, of which sugars 2g; Fat 9.7g, of which saturates 3.6g; Cholesterol 137mg; Calcium 15mg; Fibre 0g; Sodium 140mg.

Hungarian cholent

A traditional Sabbath dish of the Ashkenazi Jews, cholent is a long-simmered dish of beans, grains, meat and vegetables. The addition of whole boiled eggs is a classic feature.

SERVES 4

250g/9oz/1¹/₃ cups dried haricot
   (navy) beans
30ml/2 tbsp olive oil
1 onion, chopped
2 baking potatoes
675g/1¹/₂lb mixture of beef brisket,
   stewing beef and smoked beef
4 garlic cloves, finely chopped
50g/2oz pearl barley
15ml/1 tbsp ground paprika
pinch of cayenne pepper
1 celery stick, chopped
400g/14oz can chopped tomatoes
3 carrots, sliced
1 small turnip, diced
1 litre/1³/₄ pints/4 cups beef stock
30ml/2 tbsp white rice
4 eggs, at room temperature
salt and ground black pepper

1 Place the beans in a large bowl. Pour over plenty of cold water to cover and leave to soak for at least 8 hours. Drain the beans, then place them in a large pan, cover with fresh cold water and bring to the boil. Boil for 10 minutes, skimming off any froth that rises to the surface, then drain well and set aside.

2 Meanwhile, heat the oil in a pan, add the onion and cook gently for about 10 minutes, or until soft. Transfer the onions to the cooking pot. Peel the potatoes and cut into chunks and cut the beef into cubes.

3 Add the potatoes and beef to the pot along with the garlic, beans, barley, paprika, cayenne pepper, celery, tomatoes, carrots, turnip and stock and stir to combine. Cover and cook on low for 5–6 hours, or until the meat and vegetables are tender. Add the rice, stir, and season with salt and pepper.

4 Rinse the eggs in tepid water, then lower them into the hot stock. Cover and cook for a further 45 minutes, or until the rice is cooked. Serve hot.

Nutritional information per portion: Energy 860Kcal/3607kJ; Protein 58.9g; Carbohydrate 74.2g, of which sugars 13.7g; Fat 38.8g, of which saturates 12.7g; Cholesterol 341mg; Calcium 164mg; Fibre 10.9g; Sodium 639mg.

Beef and mushroom pudding

Based on a great British classic, this steamed savoury pudding has a light herb pastry crust made with a mixture of suet and butter for both taste and colour. A mouthwatering mixture of dried porcini and chestnut mushrooms gives the filling an intense flavour.

SERVES 4

25g/1oz/¹/₂ cup dried porcini mushrooms
475ml/16fl oz/2 cups near-boiling stock
60ml/4 tbsp plain (all-purpose) flour
675g/1¹/₂lb stewing steak, trimmed and
   cut into 2cm/³/₄in pieces
45ml/3 tbsp sunflower oil
1 large onion, finely chopped
225g/8oz chestnut or flat mushrooms,
   thickly sliced
1 bay leaf
15ml/1 tbsp Worcestershire sauce
75ml/2¹/₂fl oz/¹/₃ cup port or red wine
salt and ground black pepper

FOR THE PASTRY

275g/10oz/2¹/₂ cups self-raising
   (self-rising) flour
2.5ml/¹/₂ tsp baking powder
2.5ml/¹/₂ tsp salt
15ml/1 tbsp each chopped parsley and
   fresh thyme
75g/3oz/1¹/₂ cups beef or vegetable suet
   (chilled, grated shortening)
50g/2oz/¹/₄ cup butter, frozen and
   grated
1 egg, lightly beaten
about 150ml/¹/₄ pint/²/₃ cup cold water

1 Put the dried mushrooms in a bowl and pour over the stock. Leave to soak for about 20 minutes.

2 Meanwhile, place the flour in a bowl, season, then add the meat and toss to coat. Heat the oil in a frying pan and fry the meat in batches until browned. Transfer to the cooking pot. Add the onion to the pan and cook for 10 minutes, or until softened. Transfer to the cooking pot, then add the chestnut mushrooms and bay leaf.

3 Combine the Worcestershire sauce with the port, then pour into the pot. Drain the porcini mushrooms, pouring the stock into the pot, then chop them and add to the pot. Stir, cover and cook on high or auto for 1 hour. Reduce the heat to low and cook for 5–6 hours, or until the meat is tender. Remove the bay leaf, then cool completely.

4 Butter a deep 1.7 litre/3 pint/7¹/₂ cup pudding basin. Sift the flour, baking powder and salt into a bowl and stir in the herbs, suet and butter. Make a well, add the egg and enough cold water to mix to a soft dough. Knead on a floured surface until smooth. Cut off a quarter of the dough and shape the rest into a ball. Roll out into a round large enough to line the basin. Place the pastry in the basin, allowing the excess to fall over the sides. Roll out the reserved pastry to make a lid.

5 Spoon in the filling and enough of the gravy to come to within 1cm/½in of the rim. Brush the top edge of the pastry with water and place the lid on top. Press the edges together to seal and trim off any excess.

6 Cover the basin with a pleated, double thickness layer of baking parchment and secure under the rim using string. Cover with pleated foil.

7 Put an inverted saucer or metal pastry ring in the base of the cooking pot and place the basin on top. Pour in enough near-boiling water to come just over halfway up the sides of the basin. Cover and cook on high for 3 hours. Serve.

Nutritional information per portion: Energy 1061Kcal/4444kJ; Protein 70g; Carbohydrate 75.1g, of which sugars 4.8g; Fat 54.3g, of which saturates 24.5g; Cholesterol 265mg; Calcium 319mg; Fibre 4.4g; Sodium 941mg.

Pork and potato hot-pot

Long, slow cooking makes the pork chops meltingly tender and allows the potato slices to soak up all the delicious juices from the meat. Perfect for a family meal or casual supper with friends.

SERVES 4

25g/1oz/2 tbsp butter
15ml/1 tbsp oil
1 large onion, very thinly sliced
1 garlic clove, crushed
225g/8oz/generous 3 cups button
    (white) mushrooms, sliced
1.5ml/1/4 tsp dried mixed herbs
900g/2lb potatoes, thinly sliced
4 thick pork chops, trimmed
750ml/1 1/4 pints/3 cups vegetable or
    chicken stock
salt and ground black pepper

1 Use 15g/1/2oz/1 tbsp of the butter to grease the base and halfway up the sides of the cooking pot. Heat the oil in a frying pan, add the onion and cook for 5 minutes, until softened and translucent.

2 Add the garlic and mushrooms and cook for 5 minutes until soft. Remove from the heat and stir in the mixed herbs.

3 Spoon half the mushroom mixture into the base of the cooking pot, then arrange half the potato slices on top and season.

4 Place the pork chops on top of the potatoes in a single layer. Pour about half the stock over the top to cover the potatoes.

5 Repeat the layers of the mushroom mixture and potatoes, finishing with a layer of potatoes. Pour over the remaining stock. Dot the remaining butter on top of the potatoes and cover with the lid.

6 Cook on high for 4–5 hours, or until the potatoes and meat are tender when pierced with a thin skewer.

Nutritional information per portion: Energy 511Kcal/2132kJ; Protein 17.9g; Carbohydrate 41.5g, of which sugars 6.5g; Fat 31.5g, of which saturates 12.1g; Cholesterol 67mg; Calcium 40mg; Fibre 3.7g; Sodium 529mg.

Pork fillets with prune stuffing

The sweet flavour and rich texture of dried fruit, such as prunes, goes particularly well with pork.
If you want to ring the changes, dried apricots or figs can be used instead.

SERVES 4

15g/1/2oz/1 tbsp butter
1 shallot, very finely chopped
1 stick celery, very finely chopped
finely grated rind of 1/2 orange
115g/4oz/1/2 cup (about 12) stoned
    (pitted), ready-to-eat prunes, chopped
25g/1oz/1/2 cup fresh white breadcrumbs
30ml/2 tbsp chopped fresh parsley
pinch of grated nutmeg
2 x 225g/8oz pork fillets, trimmed
6 slices Parma ham or prosciutto
15ml/1 tbsp olive oil
150ml/1/4 pint/2/3 cup dry white wine
salt and ground black pepper
mashed root vegetables and wilted pak
    choi (bok choy), to serve

1 Melt the butter in a frying pan, add the shallot and celery, and fry until soft. Transfer to a bowl and stir in the orange rind, prunes, breadcrumbs, parsley and nutmeg. Season and leave to cool.

2 Slice down the length of each fillet, cutting three-quarters of the way through. Open out each fillet and lay it out on a board. Cover, then bash with a rolling pin until 5mm/1/4in thick. Arrange three slices of ham on a board and place one pork fillet on top. Repeat. Divide the stuffing between the pork, then fold over to enclose the filling.

3 Wrap the ham around one stuffed pork fillet, and secure with cocktail sticks (toothpicks). Repeat with the remaining ham and fillet.

4 Heat the oil in the frying pan and brown the fillets all over, before transferring them to the cooking pot. Pour the wine into the pan and bring almost to the boil, then pour over the pork. Cover and cook on high for 1 hour, then reduce the temperature to low and cook for 2–3 hours, until the pork is cooked.

5 Serve the pork with mashed root vegetables and wilted pak choi.

Nutritional information per portion: Energy 245Kcal/1027kJ; Protein 17.3g; Carbohydrate 14.6g, of which sugars 11.3g; Fat 10.8g, of which saturates 4g; Cholesterol 59mg; Calcium 34mg; Fibre 2g; Sodium 378mg.

Italian pork sausage stew

This hearty casserole, made with spicy sausages and haricot beans, is flavoured with fragrant fresh herbs and dry Italian wine. Serve with Italian bread for mopping up the delicious juices.

SERVES 4

225g/8oz/1¼ cups dried haricot (navy)
   beans
2 sprigs fresh thyme
30ml/2 tsp olive oil
450g/1lb fresh Italian pork sausages
1 onion, finely chopped
2 sticks celery, finely diced
300ml/½ pint/1¼ cups dry red or white
   wine, preferably Italian
1 sprig of fresh rosemary

1 bay leaf
300ml/½ pint/1¼ cups boiling
   vegetable stock
200g/7oz can chopped tomatoes
¼ head dark green cabbage such as
   cavolo nero or Savoy, finely shredded
salt and ground black pepper
chopped fresh thyme, to garnish
crusty Italian bread, to serve

1 Put the haricot beans in a large bowl and cover with cold water. Leave to soak for at least 8 hours, or overnight.

2 Drain the beans and place in a pan with the thyme sprigs and plenty of cold water. Bring to the boil and boil for 10 minutes, then drain and place in the cooking pot, discarding the thyme.

3 Heat the oil in a pan and cook the sausages until brown. Transfer to the cooking pot and discard all but 15ml/1 tbsp of the fat in the pan. Add the onion and celery to the pan and cook for 5 minutes. Add the wine, rosemary and bay leaf and bring to the boil. Pour over the sausages, add the stock and seasoning. Cover, switch to high and cook for 5–6 hours, until the beans are tender.

4 Stir the tomatoes and the cabbage into the stew. Cover and cook for 30–45 minutes until the cabbage is tender. Divide between warmed plates, garnish with chopped thyme and serve with crusty bread.

Nutritional information per portion: Energy 620Kcal/2593kJ; Protein 28.4g; Carbohydrate 47.4g, of which sugars 9.9g; Fat 30.9g, of which saturates 10.8g; Cholesterol 67.5mg; Calcium 205mg; Fibre 7.6g; Sodium 1139mg.

Spicy pork casserole with dried fruit

Inspired by the South American mole – a paste of chilli, shallots and nuts – this casserole is thickened and flavoured with a similar blend, bringing out the taste of the onions, meat and sweet dried fruit.

SERVES 6

25ml/1¹/₂ tbsp plain (all-purpose) flour
1kg/2¹/₄lb shoulder or leg of pork, cut
   into 4cm/1¹/₂in cubes
30ml/2 tbsp olive oil
450ml/³/₄ pint/scant 2 cups white wine
150ml/¹/₄ pint/²/₃ cup vegetable stock
   or water
115g/4oz/1¹/₂ cups ready-to-eat prunes
115g/4oz/1¹/₂ cups ready-to-eat dried
   apricots
grated rind and juice of 1 small orange
pinch of muscovado sugar
30ml/2 tbsp chopped fresh parsley
1 fresh green or red chilli, finely chopped
salt and ground black pepper
plain boiled rice, to serve

FOR THE MOLE

3 dried ancho chillies and 2 dried pasilla
   chillies (or other varieties of large,
   medium-hot dried red chillies)
30ml/2 tbsp olive oil
2 large onions, finely chopped
3 garlic cloves, chopped
1 fresh green chilli, seeded and
   finely chopped
10ml/2 tsp ground coriander
5ml/1 tsp mild Spanish paprika
50g/2oz/¹/₂ cup blanched almonds,
   toasted
15ml/1 tbsp chopped fresh oregano

1 Make the mole paste first. Toast the dried chillies in a dry frying pan over a low heat for 1–2 minutes, stirring, until they are aromatic. Place the chillies in a bowl, pour over warm water to cover and soak for about 30 minutes.

2 Drain the chillies, reserving the soaking water, then remove and discard the stalks and seeds. Heat the oil in a frying pan and fry the onions for 10 minutes until soft. Remove two-thirds of the onions and set aside. Add the garlic, fresh chilli and ground coriander to the pan and cook for 5 minutes.

3 Process the onion mixture in a food processor with the drained chillies, paprika, almonds, oregano and 45–60ml/3–4 tbsp of the soaking liquid to make a paste.

4 Place the flour in a shallow dish and season. Add the pork and toss to coat. Wipe the frying pan clean and heat the oil. Fry the pork over a high heat for 5–6 minutes, stirring, until sealed on all sides. Transfer the pork to the cooking pot and switch the cooker to high.

5 Add the reserved onions to the pan. Pour in the white wine and the vegetable stock and simmer for 1 minute. Stir in half the mole paste, bring back to the boil and bubble for a few seconds before pouring over the pork. Stir, then cover and cook for 2 hours.

6 Stir the prunes, dried apricots, orange juice and sugar into the stew. Switch the cooker to low and cook for 2–3 hours, or until the pork is very tender. Stir in the remaining mole paste and cook for 30 minutes. Garnish with orange rind, parsley and chilli and serve with rice.

Nutritional information per portion: Energy 477Kcal/1999kJ; Protein 40.7g; Carbohydrate 25.6g, of which sugars 21g; Fat 19.1g, of which saturates 3.8g; Cholesterol 105mg; Calcium 86mg; Fibre 4.1g; Sodium 149mg.

Potato and sausage casserole

There are many variations of this traditional Irish supper dish, known as Irish coddle, but the basic ingredients are the same wherever you go – potatoes, sausages and bacon.

SERVES 4

15ml/1 tbsp vegetable oil

8 large pork sausages

4 bacon rashers (strips), cut into 2.5cm/
   1in pieces

1 large onion, chopped

2 garlic cloves, crushed

4 large baking potatoes, peeled and
   thinly sliced

1.5ml/¼ tsp fresh sage

300ml/½ pint/1¼ cups vegetable or
   chicken stock

salt and ground black pepper

1 Heat the oil in a frying pan. Gently fry the sausages for 5 minutes, turning frequently until they are golden but not cooked through. Set aside. Discard all but 10ml/2 tsp of fat from the pan.

2 Add the bacon to the pan and fry for 2 minutes. Add the onion and fry for about 8 minutes, stirring frequently until golden. Add the garlic and fry for a further 1 minute, then turn off the heat.

3 Arrange half the potato in the base of the cooking pot. Spoon the bacon and onion mixture on top. Season well with salt and pepper, and sprinkle with the fresh sage. Cover with the remaining potato.

4 Pour the stock over the potatoes and top with the sausages. Cover with the lid and cook on high for 3–4 hours, or until the potatoes are tender and the sausages cooked through. Serve hot.

Nutritional information per portion: Energy 717Kcal/2984kJ; Protein 20.5g; Carbohydrate 49.9g, of which sugars 6.1g; Fat 49.8g, of which saturates 18.1g; Cholesterol 78.1mg; Calcium 73mg; Fibre 4g; Sodium 1322mg.

Boston baked beans

The slow cooker was actually invented for making baked beans. Molasses gives the beans a very rich flavour and dark colour, but you can replace it with maple syrup if you prefer.

SERVES 8

450g/1lb/2¹/₂ cups dried haricot
    (navy) beans
4 whole cloves
2 onions, peeled
1 bay leaf
90ml/6 tbsp tomato ketchup
30ml/2 tbsp molasses
30ml/2 tbsp dark brown sugar
15ml/1tbsp Dijon-style mustard
475ml/16fl oz/2 cups unsalted
    vegetable stock
225g/8oz piece of salt pork
salt and ground black pepper

1 Rinse the beans, then place in a large bowl. Cover with cold water and soak for at least 8 hours.

2 Drain and rinse the beans and place in a pan. Cover with water and bring to the boil. Boil for 10 minutes, then drain and transfer to the cooking pot. Stick two cloves in each onion and add to the pot with the bay leaf.

3 Mix the ketchup, molasses, sugar, mustard and stock together and pour over the beans. Add more stock, if necessary, so that the beans are almost covered with liquid.

4 Cover and switch the cooker to low. Cook for 3 hours.

5 Towards the end of cooking time, put the pork in a pan of boiling water and cook for 3 minutes. Score the rind. Add the pork to the pot, pushing it down below the surface, skin side up. Cook for 5–6 hours, until the beans are tender.

6 Remove the pork and cool slightly. Slice off the rind and fat and slice the meat. Skim off the fat from the top of the beans, then stir in the meat. Season and serve hot.

Nutritional information per portion: Energy 228Kcal/968kJ; Protein 13.4g; Carbohydrate 43.9g, of which sugars 19.4g; Fat 1g, of which saturates 0.1g; Cholesterol 0mg; Calcium 140mg; Fibre 9.5g; Sodium 334mg.

Cider-glazed gammon

This is a classic buffet centrepiece, which is ideal for Christmas or Thanksgiving. A fresh cranberry sauce provides the perfect foil to the richness of the meat.

SERVES 8

2kg/4¹/₂lb middle gammon joint, soaked
   overnight, if smoked
2 small onions
about 30 whole cloves
3 bay leaves
10 black peppercorns
150ml/¹/₄ pint/²/₃ cup medium-dry
   (medium-hard) cider
45ml/3 tbsp soft light brown sugar

FOR THE CRANBERRY SAUCE
350g/12oz/3 cups cranberries
175g/6oz/scant 1 cup caster
   (superfine) sugar
grated rind and juice of 2 clementines
30ml/2 tbsp port

1 Drain the gammon, if soaked overnight, then place in the cooking pot. Stud the onions with six of the cloves and add to the cooking pot with the bay leaves and peppercorns. Pour over enough water to just cover the gammon. Switch the cooker to high, cover and cook for 1 hour.

2 Skim off any scum, re-cover and cook for 4–5 hours. Check once during cooking and skim the surface, if necessary. Place the gammon in a roasting pan or ovenproof dish and leave for 15 minutes until cool enough to handle.

3 Pour the cider into a pan, add the brown sugar and heat, stirring, until dissolved. Simmer for 5 minutes to make a sticky glaze, then cool for a few minutes so that it thickens slightly.

4 Preheat the oven to 220°C/425°F/Gas 7. Snip the string off the gammon then slice off the rind, leaving a thin layer of fat over the meat and score the fat into a diamond pattern. Press a clove into the centre of each diamond, then spoon over the glaze. Bake for 25 minutes until the fat is brown.

5 Meanwhile, make the cranberry sauce. Wash the pot, then add all the ingredients for the cranberry sauce. Switch to high and cook uncovered for 20 minutes, stirring, until the sugar has dissolved. Cover and cook on high for 1¹/₂–2 hours until the cranberries are tender. Serve with the gammon.

Nutritional information per portion: Energy 404Kcal/1689kJ; Protein 44.1g; Carbohydrate 15.2g, of which sugars 14.8g; Fat 18.8g, of which saturates 6.3g; Cholesterol 57mg; Calcium 25mg; Fibre 1g; Sodium 220mg.

Pork with chickpeas and orange

This winter speciality is a familiar dish in the Aegean islands, particularly in Crete. This version comes from the island of Chios. Serve this lovely dish with fresh bread and a bowl of black olives.

SERVES 4

350g/12oz/1³/₄ cups dried chickpeas,
    soaked overnight in water to cover
75–90ml/5–6 tbsp olive oil
675g/1¹/₂lb boneless leg of pork, cut into
    small cubes
1 large onion, sliced
2 garlic cloves, chopped
400g/14oz can chopped tomatoes
grated rind of 1 orange
1 small dried red chilli
salt and ground black pepper

1 Drain the chickpeas, rinse them under cold water and drain them again. Place them in a large pan. Pour in enough cold water to cover generously and boil rapidly for 10 minutes uncovered. Skim the surface. Drain the beans, reserving the cooking liquid, and transfer the beans to the cooking pot.

2 Heat the olive oil in the clean pan and brown the meat cubes in batches. As each cube browns, lift it out with a slotted spoon and put it in the cooking pot. When all the meat cubes have been browned, add the onion to the oil remaining in the pan and sauté the slices until light golden. Stir in the garlic, then as soon as it becomes aromatic, add the tomatoes and orange rind.

3 Crumble in the chilli and transfer the mixture to the cooking pot. Pour the reserved cooking liquid into the pan and bring to the boil. Add black pepper, but not salt at this stage.

4 Pour enough of the boiling liquid into the cooking pot to cover the meat and chickpeas. Switch the slow cooker to high. Cover and cook on high for 4–5 hours. Season with salt before serving.

Nutritional information per portion: Energy 663Kcal/2,781kJ; Protein 56.7g; Carbohydrate 54.4g, of which sugars 11g; Fat 25.7g, of which saturates 4.9g; Cholesterol 106mg; Calcium 184mg; Fibre 11.8g; Sodium 164mg.

Mutton hot-pot

Mutton is hard to come by today but it really is worth looking out for. Try your local farmers' market or ask your butcher if he could get it for you. It often has a superior flavour to lamb, and requires longer, slower cooking.

SERVES 6

6 mutton chops
6 lamb's kidneys
1 large onion, sliced
450g/1lb potatoes, sliced
600ml/1 pint/2½ cups dark stock
salt and ground black pepper

1 Trim the mutton chops, leaving a little fat but no bone. Slice the kidneys in two horizontally and remove the fat and core with sharp scissors.

2 Place three of the chops in the cooking pot and season well with salt and black pepper. Add a layer of half the kidneys, then half the onion and finally half the potatoes. Season lightly.

3 Repeat the process, seasoning as you go and making sure that you finish with an even layer of potatoes.

4 Heat the stock and pour it into the cooking pot, just about covering everything but leaving the potatoes just showing at the top. Cover and cook on high for 2 hours. Reduce the temperature to low and cook for 4–6 hours, or until the mutton is very tender.

Nutritional information per portion Energy 626kcal/2629kJ; Protein 76.9g; Carbohydrate 23.1g, of which sugars 5g; Fat 25.8g, of which saturates 11.6g; Cholesterol 374mg; Calcium 76mg; Fibre 2g; Sodium 269mg.

Moroccan lamb with honey and prunes

This classic dish of the Moroccan Jews is eaten at Rosh Hashanah – the Jewish New Year – when sweet foods are served in anticipation of a sweet new year to come.

SERVES 6

130g/4¹/₂oz/generous ¹/₂ cup stoned (pitted) prunes
350ml/12fl oz/1¹/₂ cups hot tea
1kg/2¹/₄lb stewing or braising lamb
30ml/2 tbsp olive oil
1 onion, chopped
2.5ml/¹/₂ tsp ground ginger
2.5ml/¹/₂ tsp curry powder
pinch of freshly grated nutmeg
10ml/2 tsp ground cinnamon
1.5ml/¹/₄ tsp saffron threads
30ml/2 tbsp hot water
75ml/5 tbsp clear honey
200ml/7fl oz/scant 1 cup near-boiling lamb or beef stock
salt and ground black pepper
115g/4oz/1 cup blanched almonds, toasted
30ml/2 tbsp chopped fresh coriander (cilantro) and 3 hard-boiled eggs, cut into wedges, to garnish

1 Put the prunes in a heatproof bowl, then pour over the tea and leave to soak. Meanwhile, trim the lamb and cut into chunky pieces. Heat the oil in a frying pan and sauté the lamb in batches for 5 minutes until browned. Remove with a slotted spoon and transfer to the cooking pot.

2 Add the onion to the frying pan and cook for 5 minutes, until starting to soften. Stir in the ginger, curry powder, nutmeg, cinnamon, salt and a large pinch of pepper, and cook for 1 minute. Add to the cooking pot with the meat and their juices.

3 Drain the prunes, adding the soaking liquid to the lamb. Cover the prunes. Soak the saffron in the hot water for 1 minute, then add to the pot with the honey and stock. Cover and cook on high or auto for 1 hour. Reduce the temperature to low and cook for 5–7 hours, or until the lamb is very tender.

4 Add the prunes to the pot and stir to mix. Cook for 30 minutes, or until warmed through. Serve sprinkled with the toasted almonds and chopped coriander, and topped with the wedges of hard-boiled egg.

Nutritional information per portion: Energy 490Kcal/2051kJ; Protein 43.6g; Carbohydrate 23.8g, of which sugars 23.4g; Fat 25.2g, of which saturates 10.3g; Cholesterol 279mg; Calcium 41mg; Fibre 1.4g; Sodium 197mg.

Lamb in dill sauce

In this recipe, the lamb is cooked with vegetables to make a clear well-flavoured broth, which is then thickened with an egg and cream mixture to make a smooth delicate sauce.

SERVES 6

1.3kg/3lb lean boneless lamb
1 small onion, trimmed and quartered
1 carrot, thickly sliced
1 bay leaf
4 sprigs of fresh dill, plus 45ml/3 tbsp
    chopped
1 thinly pared strip of lemon rind
750ml/1¼ pints/3 cups boiling stock
15ml/1 tbsp olive oil
15g/¹/₂oz/1 tbsp unsalted (sweet) butter
225g/8oz small shallots, peeled
15ml/1 tbsp plain (all-purpose) flour
115g/4oz frozen petits pois, defrosted
1 egg yolk
75ml/2¹/₂fl oz/¹/₃ cup single (light)
    cream, at room temperature
salt and ground black pepper
new potatoes and carrots, to serve

1 Trim the lamb and cut into 2.5cm/1in pieces. Place in the cooking pot with the onion, carrot, bay leaf, dill sprigs and lemon rind. Pour over the stock, cover and cook on high for 1 hour. Skim off any scum, then re-cover and cook for a further 2 hours on high or 4 hours on low, until the lamb is fairly tender.

2 Remove the meat from the pot. Strain the stock, discarding the vegetables and herbs. Clean the cooking pot. Return the meat and half the stock (reserving the rest) to the pot, cover and switch to high.

3 Heat the oil and butter in a pan, add the shallots and cook gently for 10–15 minutes, or until browned and tender. Transfer the shallots to the pot.

4 Sprinkle the flour over the fat remaining in the pan, then slowly stir in the reserved stock. Bring to the boil, stirring until thickened, then stir into the lamb mixture. Stir in the peas and season. Cook on high for 30 minutes until hot. Blend the egg yolk and cream together, then stir in a few spoonfuls of the stock. Add to the casserole in a thin stream, stirring until slightly thickened. Stir in the chopped dill and serve with potatoes and carrots.

Nutritional information per portion: Energy 631Kcal/2629kJ; Protein 60.9g; Carbohydrate 7g, of which sugars 3.5g; Fat 40g, of which saturates 17.5g; Cholesterol 249mg; Calcium 123mg; Fibre 1.9g; Sodium 566mg.

Lancashire hot-pot

This dish is traditionally made without browning the lamb or vegetables, and relies on long, slow cooking to develop the flavour. You can brown the top under the grill, if you like.

SERVES 4

900g/2lb potatoes, thinly sliced

2 onions, peeled and sliced

2 carrots, peeled and sliced

1 stick celery, trimmed and sliced

1 leek, peeled and sliced

225g/8oz/generous 3 cups button (white) mushrooms, sliced

5ml/1 tsp dried mixed herbs

8 middle neck or loin lamb chops, about 900g/2lb in total weight, trimmed

small sprig of rosemary

475ml/16fl oz/2 cups lamb or beef stock

15g/¹/₂oz/1 tbsp butter, melted

salt and ground black pepper

1 Place a layer of sliced potatoes in the base of the cooking pot, and top with some sliced vegetables and a sprinkling of dried herbs, salt and pepper. Put four of the chops on top.

2 Repeat the layers of sliced potato, vegetables, dried herbs and meat, tucking the rosemary sprig down the side of the cooking pot. Continue layering up the remaining vegetables, and finishing with a neat layer of sliced potatoes on the top.

3 Pour the meat stock into the cooking pot, then cover with the lid and switch the slow cooker to high or auto. Cook for 1 hour, then reduce the temperature to low or leave on auto and cook for 6–8 hours or until tender.

4 Brush the top layer of potatoes with melted butter. Place under a preheated grill (broiler) and cook for 5 minutes, or until the potatoes are lightly browned. Serve immediately.

Nutritional information per portion: Energy 850Kcal/3544kJ; Protein 44.7g; Carbohydrate 45.3g, of which sugars 10.1g; Fat 55.8g, of which saturates 26.5g; Cholesterol 186mg; Calcium 72mg; Fibre 4.3g; Sodium 274mg.

Lamb pie with mustard thatch

Here, a traditional shepherd's pie is given a contemporary twist with a tangy topping of mashed potato flavoured with peppery mustard. Serve with vegetables.

SERVES 4

450g/1lb lean minced (ground) lamb
1 onion, very finely chopped
2 celery sticks, thinly sliced
2 carrots, finely diced
15ml/1 tbsp cornflour (cornstarch)
   blended into 150ml/¼ pint/²/₃ cup
   lamb stock
15ml/1 tbsp Worcestershire sauce
30ml/2 tbsp chopped fresh rosemary
800g/1¾lb floury potatoes, diced
60ml/4 tbsp milk
15ml/1 tbsp wholegrain mustard
25g/1oz/2 tbsp butter
salt and ground black pepper

1 Heat a non-stick frying pan, then add the lamb and cook until lightly browned. Add the onion, celery and carrots and cook for 2–3 minutes.

2 Stir the stock and cornflour mixture into the pan. Bring to the boil, stirring, then remove from the heat. Stir in the Worcestershire sauce and rosemary, and season.

3 Transfer the mixture to the cooking pot and switch the cooker to high. Cover and cook for 3 hours.

4 Towards the end of the cooking time, cook the potatoes in a large pan of boiling salted water until tender. Drain well, mash, and stir in the milk, mustard and butter. Season to taste.

5 Spoon the mashed potatoes on top of the lamb, spreading the mixture out evenly. Cook for a further 45 minutes. Brown the topping under a pre-heated grill (broiler) for a few minutes, if you like, then serve immediately.

Nutritional information per portion: Energy 458Kcal/1920kJ; Protein 26.5g; Carbohydrate 42.2g, of which sugars 8.1g; Fat 21.5g, of which saturates 10.6g; Cholesterol 101mg; Calcium 84mg; Fibre 3.5g; Sodium 264mg.

Moussaka

This classic Greek dish is delicious in summer or winter, served with a crisp leafy salad. Try to find small, sweet aubergines with firm, shiny skins because they have the best flavour. For an authentic touch, use Kefolotiri cheese, although Cheddar cheese will give equally good results.

SERVES 6

900g/2lb small or medium aubergines (eggplants), thinly sliced
60ml/4 tbsp olive oil
1 onion, finely chopped
2 garlic cloves, crushed
450g/1lb lean minced (ground) lamb
400g/14oz can chopped tomatoes
5ml/1 tsp dried oregano
pinch of ground cinnamon
salt and ground black pepper

FOR THE TOPPING

50g/2oz/¼ cup butter
50g/2oz/½ cup plain (all-purpose) flour
600ml/1 pint/2½ cups milk
pinch of freshly grated nutmeg
75g/3oz/¾ cup grated Kefolotiri or mature Cheddar cheese
1 egg yolk
30ml/2 tbsp fresh white breadcrumbs

1 Layer the aubergine in a colander, sprinkling each layer with salt. Place over a bowl and leave for 20 minutes. Rinse and pat dry with kitchen paper. Brush the aubergine with about half the oil, then arrange the slices in a single layer on a baking sheet. Place under a medium grill (broiler) and cook, turning once, until the aubergine is softened and golden. Arrange half the aubergine in the base of the cooking pot and switch the cooker to high.

2 Heat the remaining oil in a pan, add the onion and fry for 10 minutes until soft. Add the garlic and lamb and cook until the meat is browned. Stir in the tomatoes, oregano and cinnamon, season and slowly bring to the boil. Spoon the mixture into the slow cooker, covering the aubergine. Arrange the remaining aubergine on top, then cover and cook for 2 hours.

3 Meanwhile, make the topping. Melt the butter in a pan, stir in the flour and cook for 1 minute. Stir in the milk, bring to the boil and cook until thick. Lower the heat and simmer for 1 minute. Season, then stir in the nutmeg and two-thirds of the cheese. Cool for 5 minutes, then beat in the egg yolk. Pour the sauce over the aubergine. Cover and cook for 2 hours, or until the topping is lightly set. Sprinkle the remaining cheese and the breadcrumbs over the top and cook under a grill (broiler) for 3–4 minutes until golden brown. Leave for 5–10 minutes before serving.

Nutritional information per portion: Energy 444Kcal/1850kJ; Protein 24.1g; Carbohydrate 1.5g, of which sugars 11.2g; Fat 31g, of which saturates 14g; Cholesterol 93.5mg; Calcium 268mg; Fibre 4.1g; Sodium 266mg.

Lamb shanks with cannellini beans

Earthy and substantial, this is the ideal dish for chilly autumn evenings. The beans acquire layers of taste when slow-cooked in the rich sauce provided by the meat.

SERVES 4–6

225g/8oz/1¼ cups dried cannellini
    beans, soaked overnight in water
    to cover
4 lamb shanks
30ml/2 tbsp plain (all-purpose) flour
60ml/4 tbsp olive oil
1 large onion, chopped
2 garlic cloves, sliced
1 celery stick, sliced
1 carrot, sliced
leaves from 2 fresh rosemary sprigs
2 bay leaves
175ml/6fl oz/¾ cup white wine
30ml/2 tbsp tomato purée (paste)
600ml/1 pint/2½ cups hot water
salt and ground black pepper

1 Drain the soaked beans and place in a large pan. Cover with fresh cold water, bring to the boil and boil rapidly for 10 minutes uncovered. Drain the beans and place in the cooking pot.

2 Season the lamb shanks and coat them lightly in flour. Heat the oil in a large frying pan over a high heat and brown the meat on all sides. Transfer them to the cooking pot and switch the slow cooker to high.

3 Add the onion to the oil remaining in the pan and sauté gently. As soon as it is light golden, stir in the garlic, celery, carrot, rosemary and bay leaves.

4 Pour in the wine and let it bubble and reduce, then stir in the tomato purée diluted in the hot water. Bring to the boil, season with salt and pepper and transfer to the cooking pot. Cover and cook for 4–5 hours. Season with salt before serving.

Nutritional information per portion: Energy 588Kcal/2,465kJ; Protein 43.9g; Carbohydrate 39.9g, of which sugars 6.7g; Fat 26.2g, of which saturates 9.1g; Cholesterol 114mg; Calcium 110mg; Fibre 10.5g; Sodium 161mg.

Lamb and carrot casserole with barley

Barley and carrots make natural partners for lamb and mutton. In this convenient casserole the barley extends the meat and adds to the flavour and texture, as well as thickening the sauce.

SERVES 6

675g/1¹/₂lb stewing lamb
15ml/1 tbsp vegetable oil
2 onions, sliced
675g/1¹/₂lb carrots, thickly sliced
4–6 celery sticks, sliced
45ml/3 tbsp pearl barley, rinsed
600ml/1 pint/2¹/₂ cups near-boiling lamb
     or vegetable stock
5ml/1 tsp fresh thyme leaves or pinch of
     dried mixed herbs
salt and ground black pepper
spring cabbage and jacket potatoes,
     to serve

1 Trim all excess fat from the lamb, then cut the meat into 3cm/1¹/₄in pieces. Heat the oil in a frying pan, add the lamb and fry until browned. Remove from the pan with a slotted spoon and set aside.

2 Add the onions to the pan and fry for 5 minutes until golden. Add the carrots and celery and cook for 3–4 minutes or until beginning to soften. Transfer to the cooking pot and switch the slow cooker to high.

3 Sprinkle the pearl barley over the vegetables in the cooking pot, then arrange the lamb pieces on top. Lightly season, then scatter with the herbs. Pour the stock over the meat, so that all of the meat is covered.

4 Cover with the lid and cook on auto or high for 2 hours. Skim off any scum that has risen to the surface. Re-cover the pot and leave on auto or switch to low and cook for a further 4–6 hours or until the meat, vegetables and barley are tender. Serve with spring cabbage and jacket potatoes.

Nutritional information per portion: Energy 304Kcal/1263kJ; Protein 23.2g; Carbohydrate 13g, of which sugars 11.3g; Fat 18g, of which saturates 7.5g; Cholesterol 84mg; Calcium 53mg; Fibre 3.6g; Sodium 110mg.

Tuscan pot-roasted shoulder of lamb

This delicious boned and rolled shoulder of lamb, studded with rosemary sprigs and garlic, then cooked on a bed of vegetables, makes a perfect alternative to a traditional meat roast. Check that the lamb will fit comfortably in the slow cooker before you start.

SERVES 6

15ml/1 tbsp olive oil

1.3kg/3lb lamb shoulder, trimmed, boned and tied

3 large garlic cloves

12 small fresh rosemary sprigs

115g/4oz lean rinded smoked bacon, chopped

1 onion, chopped

3 carrots, finely chopped

3 celery sticks, finely chopped

1 leek, finely chopped

150ml/¼ pint/⅔ cup red wine

300ml/½ pint/1¼ cups lamb or vegetable stock

400g/14oz can chopped tomatoes

3 sprigs of fresh thyme

2 bay leaves

400g/14oz can cannellini beans, drained and rinsed

salt and ground black pepper

potatoes or warm crusty bread, to serve

1 Heat the oil in a large frying pan and brown the lamb on all sides. Leave to stand until it is cool enough to handle.

2 Cut the garlic cloves into quarters. When the lamb is cool enough, make twelve deep incisions all over the meat. Push a piece of garlic and a sprig of rosemary into each incision.

3 Add the bacon, onion, carrot, celery and leek to the pan and cook for 10 minutes until soft, then transfer to the cooking pot. Stir the red wine into the ceramic cooking pot.

4 Add the stock and tomatoes to the pot and season. Add the thyme and bay leaves, submerging them in the liquid. Place the lamb on top, cover and cook on high for 4 hours.

5 Lift the lamb out of the pot and stir the beans into the vegetable mixture. Return the lamb, re-cover and cook for a further 1–2 hours, or until the lamb is cooked and tender.

6 Remove the lamb from the cooking pot using slotted spoons, cover with foil and leave to rest for 10 minutes. Remove the string from the lamb and carve the meat into thick slices. Remove the thyme and bay leaves from the vegetable and bean mixture and skim off any fat from the surface. Spoon the vegetables on to plates and arrange the sliced lamb on top. Serve with potatoes or bread.

Nutritional information per portion: Energy 710Kcal/2958kJ; Protein 60.2g; Carbohydrate 13.7g, of which sugars 4.8g; Fat 44.6g, of which saturates 19.4g; Cholesterol 229mg; Calcium 58mg; Fibre 4.7g; Sodium 864mg.

Vegetarian dishes

This chapter makes use of all kinds of

wonderful vegetables, beans and grains

to make fabulous slow-cooked main

meals that will appeal just as much to

meat eaters as they do to vegetarians.

Whatever you are in the mood for, you

are sure to find the perfect meat-free

recipe in this chapter.

Slow-cooked okra with tomatoes

Okra makes a deliciously sweet casserole and, as far as vegetable dishes go, this is one of the best. Made with fresh tomatoes, at the height of the summer, it is certainly a favourite lunch, especially when served with a fresh-tasting feta cheese and crusty bread.

SERVES 4

675g/1¹/₂lb fresh okra
150ml/¹/₄ pint/²/₃ cup olive oil
1 large onion, sliced
675g/1¹/₂lb fresh tomatoes, sliced,
    or 400g/14oz can chopped tomatoes
2.5ml/¹/₂ tsp sugar
30ml/2 tbsp finely chopped flat-leaf
    parsley
salt and ground black pepper

1 Cut off the conical head from each okra pod, without cutting into the body of the okra. Remove the black tip at the other end and rinse the pod.

2 Heat the oil in a large, deep pan or sauté pan and fry the onion slices until light golden. Stir in the fresh or canned tomatoes, with the sugar, and salt and pepper to taste. Cook for 5 minutes.

3 Add the okra and shake the pan to distribute them evenly and coat them in the sauce. The okra should be completely immersed in the sauce, so add enough hot water to cover.

4 Transfer to the cooking pot. Switch the slow cooker to high. Cover and cook for 3–4 hours. Add the chopped flat-leaf parsley just before serving.

Nutritional information per portion: Energy 326Kcal/1,350kJ; Protein 6.5g; Carbohydrate 14.8g, of which sugars 12.8g; Fat 27.3g, of which saturates 4.3g; Cholesterol 0mg; Calcium 295mg; Fibre 9.1g; Sodium 30mg.

Sweet and sour mixed-bean hot-pot

This dish, topped with sliced potatoes, is very easy to prepare, making the most of dried and canned ingredients from the cupboard and combining them with a rich and tangy sauce.

SERVES 6

175g/6oz green beans
40g/1¹/₂oz/3 tbsp butter
4 shallots, peeled and finely chopped
40g/1¹/₂oz/¹/₃ cup plain (all-purpose) or wholemeal (whole-wheat) flour
300ml/¹/₂ pint/1¹/₄ cups passata (bottled strained tomatoes)
120ml/4fl oz/¹/₂ cup apple juice
60ml/4 tbsp soft light brown sugar
60ml/4 tbsp tomato ketchup
60ml/4 tbsp dry sherry
60ml/4 tbsp cider vinegar
60ml/4 tbsp light soy sauce
400g/14oz can butter (lima) beans
400g/14oz can cannellini beans
400g/14oz can chickpeas
225g/8oz/3 cups mushrooms, sliced
450g/1lb unpeeled potatoes
15ml/1 tbsp olive oil
15ml/1 tbsp chopped fresh thyme
15ml/1 tbsp fresh marjoram
salt and ground black pepper
fresh herbs, to garnish

1 Cut the green beans into 2.5cm/1in lengths and set aside. Melt the butter in a pan, add the shallots and fry for 5–6 minutes, until soft. Add the flour and cook for 1 minute, stirring, then stir in the passata.

2 Add the apple juice, sugar, tomato ketchup, sherry, vinegar and light soy sauce to the pan and stir in. Bring to the boil, stirring until it thickens.

3 Rinse the beans and chickpeas and drain well. Place them in the cooking pot with the reserved green beans and mushrooms and pour over the sauce. Stir well, then cover with the lid and cook on high for 3 hours.

4 Meanwhile, thinly slice the potatoes and par-boil them for 4 minutes. Drain well, then toss them in the oil so that they are lightly coated all over.

5 Stir the fresh thyme and marjoram into the bean mixture and season to taste with black pepper. Arrange the potato slices on top of the beans, overlapping them slightly so that they cover them. Cover the pot and cook for a further 2 hours, or until the potatoes are tender.

6 Place the ceramic cooking pot under a medium grill (broiler) and cook for 4–5 minutes to brown the potato topping. Serve garnished with herbs.

Nutritional information per portion: Energy 483Kcal/2042kJ; Protein 18.5g; Carbohydrate 73.3g, of which sugars 24.8g; Fat 13.8g, of which saturates 4.5g; Cholesterol 14mg; Calcium 134mg; Fibre 10.9g; Sodium 826mg.

Mixed-bean chilli with cornbread topping

Inspired by traditional Texan cooking, this chilli combines Tex-mex with classic Texan cornbread. The delicious topping offers the starch component of the dish, making this dish a filling meal.

SERVES 4

115g/4oz/ ½ cup dried red kidney beans
115g/4oz/½ cup dried black-eyed beans
600ml/1 pint/2½ cups cold water
1 bay leaf
15ml/1 tbsp vegetable oil
1 large onion, finely chopped
1 garlic clove, crushed
5ml/1 tsp ground cumin
5ml/1 tsp chilli powder
5ml/1 tsp mild paprika
2.5ml/½ tsp dried marjoram
450g/1lb mixed vegetables, such as
   potatoes, carrots, aubergines
   (eggplants), parsnips and celery
1 vegetable stock cube
400g/14oz can chopped tomatoes
15ml/1 tbsp tomato purée (paste)
salt and ground black pepper

FOR THE CORNBREAD TOPPING
250g/9oz/2¼ cups fine cornmeal
30ml/2 tbsp wholemeal (whole-wheat)
   flour
7.5ml/1½ tsp baking powder
1 egg, plus 1 egg yolk lightly beaten
300ml/½ pint/1¼ cups milk

1 Put the dried beans in a large bowl with plenty of cold water. Leave to soak for at least 6 hours.

2 Drain and rinse the beans, then place in a pan with the cold water and the bay leaf. Bring to the boil and boil rapidly for 10 minutes. Leave to cool for a few minutes, then tip into the cooking pot and switch the slow cooker to high.

3 Heat the oil in a pan, add the onion and cook for 7–8 minutes. Add the garlic, cumin, chilli powder, paprika and marjoram and cook for 1 minute. Transfer to the pot and stir.

4 Prepare the vegetables, then cut into 2cm/¾in chunks. Add to the pot, cover and cook for 3 hours.

5 Stir the stock cube, tomatoes and tomato purée into the pot and season. Cover and cook for 30 minutes until the mixture is at boiling point. Discard the bay leaf.

6 To make the topping, combine the cornmeal, flour, baking powder and a pinch of salt. Make a well in the centre and add the egg, egg yolk and milk. Mix, then spoon over the bean mixture. Cover and cook for 1 hour, or until firm and cooked.

Nutritional information per portion: Energy 613Kcal/2595kJ; Protein 29.6g; Carbohydrate 97.4g, of which sugars 15.8g; Fat 14.5g, of which saturates 3.4g; Cholesterol 112mg; Calcium 257mg; Fibre 13.4g; Sodium 413mg.

Root vegetable casserole with caraway dumplings

Stirring soft cheese into the cooking juices gives this casserole a wonderfully creamy richness, while thickening and flavouring it at the same time. Courgette dumplings complete the meal.

SERVES 3

300ml/¹/₂ pint/1¹/₄ cups dry (hard) cider
175ml/6fl oz/³/₄ cup boiling
   vegetable stock
2 leeks
2 carrots
2 small parsnips
225g/8oz potatoes
1 sweet potato, weighing about 175g/6oz
1 bay leaf
7.5ml/1¹/₂ tsp cornflour (cornstarch)
115g/4oz full-fat soft cheese with garlic
   and herbs
salt and ground black pepper

FOR THE DUMPLINGS

115g/4oz/1 cup self-raising (self-rising)
   flour
5ml/1 tsp caraway seeds
50g/2oz/¹/₂ cup shredded vegetable suet
   (chilled, grated shortening)
1 courgette (zucchini), grated
about 75ml/5 tbsp cold water

1 Reserve 15ml/1 tbsp of the cider and pour the rest into the cooking pot with the stock. Cover with the lid and switch the cooker to high.

2 Meanwhile, prepare the vegetables. Trim the leeks and cut into 2cm/³/₄in slices. Peel the carrots, parsnips and potatoes and cut into 2cm/³/₄in chunks. Add the vegetables to the pot with the bay leaf. Cover and cook for 3 hours.

3 Blend the cornflour with the reserved cider in a bowl. Add the cheese and mix together, then gradually blend in a few spoonfuls of the cooking liquid.

4 Pour over the vegetables and stir until mixed. Season. Cover and cook for a further 1–2 hours, or until the vegetables are almost tender. Discard the bay leaf.

5 Towards the end of cooking time, make the dumplings. Sift the flour into a bowl and stir in the caraway seeds, suet, courgettes, salt and pepper. Stir in the water, adding more if necessary, to make a soft dough. Shape into 12 dumplings.

6 Place the dumplings on top of the casserole, cover and cook for 1 hour, or until the vegetables and caraway dumplings are cooked.

Nutritional information per portion: Energy 616Kcal/2584kJ; Protein 11.9g; Carbohydrate 74.9g, of which sugars 17.1g; Fat 28.9g, of which saturates 15.9g; Cholesterol 35mg; Calcium 256mg; Fibre 9.5g; Sodium 369mg.

Spicy tamarind chickpeas

Chickpeas make a good base for many vegetarian dishes. Here, they are tossed with sharp tamarind and spices to make a deliciously light vegetarian lunch or side dish.

SERVES 4

225g/8oz/1¼ cups dried chickpeas
50g/2oz tamarind pulp
45ml/3 tbsp vegetable oil
2.5ml/½ tsp cumin seeds
1 onion, very finely chopped
2 garlic cloves, crushed
2.5cm/1in piece of fresh root ginger,
   peeled and grated
5ml/1 tsp ground cumin

5ml/1 tsp ground coriander
1.5ml/¼ tsp ground turmeric
2.5ml/½ tsp salt
1 fresh green chilli, finely chopped
225g/8oz tomatoes, skinned and
   finely chopped
2.5ml/½ tsp garam masala
chopped fresh chillies and chopped onion,
   to garnish

1 Put the chickpeas in a large bowl and pour over cold water to cover. Leave to soak for at least 8 hours.

2 Drain the chickpeas and put in a pan with plenty of cold water. (Do not add salt to the water because this will toughen the chickpeas.) Bring the water to the boil and boil for at least 10 minutes. Skim off any scum, then drain the chickpeas and transfer to the cooking pot. Pour 750ml/1¼ pints/3 cups near-boiling water over the chickpeas and switch the slow cooker to high. Cover and cook for 4–5 hours until the chickpeas are just tender.

3 Towards the end of the cooking time, put the tamarind in a bowl and break up with a fork. Pour over 120ml/4fl oz/½ cup of boiling water and soak for about 15 minutes. Transfer the tamarind to a sieve (strainer) and discard the water. Rub the pulp through, discarding the stones and fibre.

4 Heat the oil in a large frying pan, add the cumin seeds and fry for 2 minutes. Add the onion, garlic and ginger and fry for 5 minutes. Add the cumin, coriander, turmeric, chilli and salt and fry for 3–4 minutes. Add the tomatoes, garam masala and tamarind pulp and bring to the boil.

5 Stir the tamarind mixture into the chickpeas, cover and cook for 1 hour. Either serve straight from the cooking pot, or spoon into a warmed serving dish and garnish with chopped chilli and onion.

Nutritional information per portion: Energy 277Kcal/1164kJ; Protein 12.8g; Carbohydrate 32.6g, of which sugars 5.3g; Fat 11.5g, of which saturates 1.3g; Cholesterol 0mg; Calcium 103mg; Fibre 7.1g; Sodium 274mg.

Savoury nut loaf

Ideal as an alternative to the traditional meat roast, this wholesome dish is perfect for special occasions. It is particularly good served with a spicy fresh tomato sauce.

SERVES 4

30ml/2 tbsp olive oil, plus extra
    for greasing
1 onion, finely chopped
1 leek, finely chopped
2 celery sticks, finely chopped
225g/8oz/3 cups mushrooms, chopped
2 garlic cloves, crushed
425g/15oz can lentils, rinsed and drained
115g/4oz/1 cup mixed nuts, such as
    hazelnuts, cashew nuts and almonds,
    finely chopped
50g/2oz/1/2 cup plain (all-purpose) flour
50g/2oz/1/2 cup grated mature (sharp)
    Cheddar cheese
1 egg, beaten
45–60ml/3–4 tbsp chopped fresh
    mixed herbs
salt and ground black pepper
chives and sprigs of fresh flat-leaf
    parsley, to garnish

1 Place an upturned saucer in the base of the cooking pot. Pour in 2.5cm/1in hot water and switch the slow cooker to high.

2 Lightly oil the base and sides of a 900g/2lb loaf tin (pan) or terrine – first making sure it will fit in the slow cooker – and line the base and sides with baking parchment.

3 Heat the oil in a pan, add the onion, leek, celery, mushrooms and garlic and cook for 10 minutes, until the vegetables have softened. Remove from the heat, then stir in the lentils, nuts and flour, cheese, egg and herbs. Season and mix well.

4 Spoon the nut mixture into the prepared loaf tin and level the surface. Cover the top with foil. Place the tin in the cooking pot and carefully pour in enough near-boiling water to come just over halfway up the side of the dish.

5 Cover the cooker and cook for about 3–4 hours, or until the loaf is firm to the touch.

6 Leave the loaf to cool in the tin for 15 minutes, then turn out on to a large serving plate. Serve the loaf hot or cold, cut into thick slices and garnished with chives and flat-leaf parsley.

Nutritional information per portion: Energy 484Kcal/2019kJ; Protein 23.7g; Carbohydrate 34.1g, of which sugars 5.1g; Fat 29g, of which saturates 5.4g; Cholesterol 69mg; Calcium 238mg; Fibre 8.7g; Sodium 128mg.

Pasta with mushrooms

Slow-cooking a mixture of mushrooms, garlic and sun-dried tomatoes together with white wine and stock makes a rich pasta sauce. Serve with chunks of fresh ciabatta bread.

SERVES 4

15g/¹/₂oz dried porcini mushrooms
120ml/4fl oz/¹/₂ cup hot water
2 cloves garlic, finely chopped
2 large pieces sun-dried tomato in olive
  oil, drained and sliced into thin strips
120ml/4fl oz/¹/₂ cup dry white wine
120ml/4fl oz/¹/₂ cup vegetable stock
225g/8oz/2 cups chestnut mushrooms,
  thinly sliced
450g/1lb/4 cups dried short pasta
  shapes, such as ruote,
  penne, fusilli or eliche
1 handful flat-leaf parsley, chopped
salt and ground black pepper
rocket (arugula) and/or fresh parsley,
  to garnish

1 Put the dried mushrooms in a large bowl. Pour over the hot water and leave to soak for 15 minutes.

2 Put the garlic, tomatoes, wine, stock and chestnut mushrooms into the cooking pot and switch the slow cooker to high.

3 Transfer the porcini mushrooms to a sieve (strainer) set over a bowl. Reserve the soaking liquid. Chop the porcini finely. Add the liquid and the porcini to the cooking pot and cover with the lid.

4 Cook on high for 1 hour, stirring halfway through cooking to ensure that the mushrooms cook evenly.

5 Switch the slow cooker to the low setting and cook for 1–2 hours, until the mushrooms are tender.

6 Cook the pasta in boiling salted water for 10 minutes. Drain the pasta and transfer to a warmed bowl. Stir the chopped parsley into the sauce and season. Add the sauce to the pasta and toss well. Serve with rocket and/or parsley.

Nutritional information per portion: Energy 420Kcal/1787kJ; Protein 15.1g; Carbohydrate 84.9g, of which sugars 5.1g; Fat 2.6g, of which saturates 0.3g; Cholesterol 0 mg; Calcium 61mg; Fibre 4.8g; Sodium 14mg.

Couscous-stuffed sweet peppers

The peppers are softened in boiling water before filling to ensure tender results. Choose red, yellow or orange peppers, but avoid green ones because they do not have such a sweet taste.

SERVES 4

4 (bell) peppers
75g/3oz/1/2 cup instant couscous
75ml/2¹/₂fl oz/¹/₃ cup boiling vegetable
   stock
15ml/1 tbsp olive oil
10ml/2 tsp white wine vinegar
50g/2oz dried apricots, finely chopped

75g/3oz feta cheese, cut into tiny cubes
3 ripe tomatoes, skinned, seeded
   and chopped
45ml/3 tbsp toasted pine nuts
30ml/2 tbsp chopped fresh parsley
salt and ground black pepper
flat-leaf parsley, to garnish

1 Halve the peppers lengthways, then remove the core and seeds. Place the peppers in a large heatproof bowl and pour over boiling water to cover. Leave to stand for about 3 minutes, then drain thoroughly and set aside.

2 Meanwhile, put the couscous in a small bowl and pour over the stock. Leave to stand for about 5 minutes until all the water has been absorbed. Using a fork, fluff up the couscous, then stir in the oil, vinegar, apricots, feta cheese, tomatoes, pine nuts and parsley, and season to taste.

3 Fill the peppers with the couscous mixture, gently packing it down using the back of a spoon.

4 Place the peppers, filling side up, in the cooking pot, then pour 150ml/¹/₄ pint/²/₃ cup near-boiling water around them.

5 Cover with the lid, switch the slow cooker to high and cook for 2–3 hours, or until the peppers are tender. Brown under a hot grill (broiler) for 2 minutes and serve garnished with fresh parsley.

Nutritional information per portion: Energy 303Kcal/1266kJ; Protein 33.7g; Carbohydrate 33.6g, of which sugars 17g; Fat 15.8g, of which saturates 3.9g; Cholesterol 13mg; Calcium 105mg; Fibre 4.3g; Sodium 285mg.

Parsnips and chickpeas in garlic, onion, chilli and ginger paste

The sweet flavour of parsnips goes well with the spices in this Indian-style stew. It makes an ideal meal for vegetarians because chickpeas are high in protein. Serve with warm Indian bread.

SERVES 4

5 garlic cloves, finely chopped
1 small onion, chopped
5cm/2in piece fresh root ginger, chopped
2 green chillies, seeded and finely chopped
75ml/5 tbsp cold water
60ml/4 tbsp groundnut (peanut) oil
5ml/1 tsp cumin seeds
10ml/2 tsp coriander seeds
5ml/1 tsp ground turmeric
2.5ml/^{1}/$_2$ tsp chilli powder or mild paprika
50g/2oz/^{1}/$_2$ cup cashew nuts, toasted
    and ground

225g/8oz tomatoes, peeled and chopped
400g/14oz can chickpeas, drained
    and rinsed
900g/2lb parsnips, peeled and cut into
    2cm/^{3}/$_4$in chunks
350ml/12 fl oz/1^1/$_2$ cups boiling vegetable
    stock
juice of 1 lime, to taste
salt and ground black pepper
chopped fresh coriander (cilantro) leaves,
    toasted cashew nuts and natural (plain)
    yogurt, to serve

1 Reserve 10ml/2 tsp of the garlic, then place the remainder in a food processor or blender with the onion, ginger and half the chilli. Add the water and process to make a smooth paste.

2 Heat the oil in a large frying pan, add the cumin seeds and cook for 30 seconds. Stir in the coriander seeds, turmeric, chilli powder or paprika and the ground cashews. Add the ginger and chilli paste and cook, stirring frequently, until the paste bubbles and the water begins to evaporate.

3 Add the tomatoes and cook for 1 minute. Transfer the mixture to the cooking pot and switch the cooker to high. Add the chickpeas and parsnips to the ceramic cooking pot and stir to coat in the spicy tomato mixture, then stir in the stock and season. Cover and cook on high for 4 hours, or until the parsnips are tender.

4 Stir half the lime juice, the reserved garlic and green chilli into the stew. Cover and cook for 30 minutes, then taste and add more lime juice if needed. Spoon on to plates and sprinkle with fresh coriander and toasted cashew nuts. Serve with natural yogurt.

Nutritional information per portion: Energy 453Kcal/1899kJ; Protein 14.8g; Carbohydrate 50.1g, of which sugars 16.6g; Fat 23g, of which saturates 4.3g; Cholesterol 0mg; Calcium 148mg; Fibre 15.8g; Sodium 394mg.

Rosemary risotto with borlotti beans

Using easy-cook Italian rice means that all the wine and stock can be added at the same time, rather than ladleful by ladleful, as with a traditional risotto.

SERVES 3

400g/14oz can borlotti beans
15g/¹/₂oz/1 tbsp butter
15ml/1 tbsp olive oil
1 onion, finely chopped
2 garlic cloves, crushed
120ml/4fl oz/¹/₂ cup dry white wine
225g/8oz/generous 1 cup easy-cook (converted) Italian rice
750ml/1¹/₄ pints/3 cups boiling vegetable stock
60ml/4 tbsp mascarpone cheese
5ml/1 tsp chopped fresh rosemary
65g/2¹/₂oz/³/₄ cup freshly grated Parmesan cheese, plus extra to serve (optional)
salt and ground black pepper

1 Drain the borlotti beans, rinse and drain again. Place two-thirds of the beans in a food processor and process to a coarse purée. Set the rest aside.

2 Heat the butter and oil in a pan, add the onion and garlic and fry for 7–8 minutes until soft. Transfer the mixture to the cooking pot and stir in the wine and bean purée. Cover and cook on high for 1 hour.

3 Add the rice then stir in the stock. Cover again and cook for 45 minutes, stirring once halfway through cooking.

4 Stir the reserved borlotti beans, mascarpone and rosemary into the risotto. Cover and cook for a further 15 minutes, until the rice is tender but still has a little bite. Stir the Parmesan cheese into the risotto and season to taste.

5 Turn off the cooker, cover and leave for about 5 minutes, so that the risotto absorbs the flavours fully and the rice completes cooking. Spoon the rice into warmed serving bowls and serve immediately, sprinkled with the extra grated Parmesan cheese.

Nutritional information per portion: Energy 651Kcal/2740kJ; Protein 25g; Carbohydrate 87g, of which sugars 4.6g; Fat 22.2g, of which saturates 10.5g; Cholesterol 41.9mg; Calcium 357mg; Fibre 7.1g; Sodium 1462mg.

Braised beans and grains

This lovely Cretan dish is easy to make, but it is vital that you start soaking the pulses and wheat the day before you want to serve it. Serve with warmed crusty bread to mop up the sauce.

SERVES 4

200g/7oz/generous 1 cup mixed dried
    beans, soaked overnight in water
25g/1oz/2 tbsp wholemeal (whole-wheat)
    grains, soaked overnight in water
150ml/¼ pint/²/₃ cup olive oil
1 large onion, finely chopped
2 garlic cloves, crushed
5 or 6 fresh sage leaves, chopped
300ml/½ pint/1¼ cups vegetable stock
juice of 1 lemon
salt and ground black pepper
3 spring onions (scallions), thinly sliced
    and 60–75ml/4–5 tbsp chopped fresh
    dill, to garnish

1 Drain the beans and wheat, rinse under cold water and place them in a large pan. Pour in enough cold water to cover generously, bring to the boil and boil rapidly for 10 minutes uncovered. Skim the surface and transfer to the cooking pot.

2 Heat the oil in a frying pan and fry the onion until light golden. Add the garlic and sage. As soon as the garlic becomes aromatic, stir in the vegetable stock, add plenty of pepper and bring to the boil. Transfer to the cooking pot and switch the slow cooker to high. Cover and cook for 4–5 hours.

3 Stir in the lemon juice and season with salt, then spoon into serving bowls, top with a sprinkling of spring onions and dill, and serve.

Nutritional information per portion: Energy 428Kcal/1,788kJ; Protein 13.4g; Carbohydrate 37.7g, of which sugars 4.3g; Fat 26g, of which saturates 3.7g; Cholesterol 0mg; Calcium 62mg; Fibre 3.7g; Sodium 24mg.

Baked eggs with creamy leeks

Enjoy these deliciously creamy eggs for a light lunch or supper with toast and a salad. You can use other vegetables in place of the leeks, such as puréed spinach or ratatouille.

SERVES 4

15g/¹/₂oz/1 tbsp butter, plus extra
    for greasing
225g/8oz small leeks, thinly sliced
60–90ml/4–6 tbsp whipping or double
    (heavy) cream
freshly grated nutmeg
4 eggs
salt and ground black pepper

1 Pour about 2.5cm/1in hot water into the cooking pot and switch the slow cooker to high.

2 Using a pastry brush, lightly grease the base and insides of four 175ml/6fl oz/³/₄ cup ramekins or individual soufflé dishes with butter.

3 Melt the butter in a small frying pan and cook the leeks over a medium heat, stirring frequently, until softened.

4 Add 45ml/3 tbsp of the cream and cook gently for about 5 minutes, or until the leeks are very soft and the cream has thickened a little. Season with salt, black pepper and nutmeg.

5 Spoon the leeks into the ramekins or soufflé dishes, dividing the mixture equally. Using the back of the spoon, make a hollow in the centre of each pile of leeks, then break an egg into the hollow. Spoon 5–10ml/1–2 tsp of the remaining cream over each egg and season lightly.

6 Cover each dish with clear film (plastic wrap) and place in the slow cooker. If necessary, pour in a little more boiling water to come halfway up the sides of the dishes. Cover and cook for 30 minutes, or until the egg whites are set and the yolks are still soft, or slightly longer if you prefer the eggs a little firmer.

Nutritional information per portion: Energy 239Kcal/990kJ; Protein 8.5g; Carbohydrate 2g, of which sugars 1.6g; Fat 21.9g, of which saturates 11.4g; Cholesterol 266mg; Calcium 58mg; Fibre 1.2g; Sodium 110mg.

Onions stuffed with goat's cheese and sun-dried tomatoes

Long, slow cooking is the best way to get maximum flavour from onions, so the slow cooker is the natural choice for this delicious dish. Serve with rice to make a great main course.

SERVES 4

2 large onions, unpeeled
30ml/2 tbsp olive oil (or use oil from the sun-dried tomatoes)
150g/5oz/²/₃ cup firm goat's cheese, crumbled or cubed
50g/2oz/1 cup fresh white breadcrumbs
8 sun-dried tomatoes in olive oil, drained and chopped
1 garlic clove, finely chopped
2.5ml/¹/₂ tsp fresh thyme
30ml/2 tbsp chopped fresh parsley
1 small egg, beaten
45ml/3 tbsp pine nuts
150ml/¹/₄ pint/²/₃ cup near-boiling vegetable stock
salt and ground black pepper
chopped fresh parsley, to garnish

1 Bring a pan of water to the boil. Add the whole onions in their skins and boil for 10 minutes. Drain the onions and leave until cool enough to handle, then cut each onion in half horizontally and peel. Using a teaspoon, remove the centre of each onion, leaving a thick shell.

2 Finely chop the flesh from one of the scooped-out onions and place in a bowl. Stir in 5ml/1 tsp of the olive oil, then add the cheese, breadcrumbs, tomatoes, garlic, thyme, parsley, egg and pine nuts. Season with the salt and ground black pepper and mix.

3 Divide the stuffing among the onions and cover each one with a piece of oiled foil. Brush the base of the cooking pot with 15ml/1 tbsp of the oil, then pour in the stock. Arrange the onions in the base of the pot, cover and cook on high for 4 hours until the onions are tender but still hold their shape.

4 Remove the onions from the cooker and transfer them to a grill (broiler) pan. Remove the foil and drizzle the tops with the remaining oil. Brown under a medium grill for 3–4 minutes. Serve, garnished with the chopped fresh parsley.

Nutritional information per portion: Energy 330Kcal/1370kJ; Protein 13.8g; Carbohydrate 14.3g, of which sugars 11.3g; Fat 24.7g, of which saturates 8.4g; Cholesterol 83.7mg; Calcium 98mg; Fibre 1.9g; Sodium 349mg.

Sweet pumpkin and peanut curry

Rich, sweet, spicy and fragrant, the flavours of this delicious Thai-style curry really come together with long, slow cooking. Serve with rice or noodles for a substantial supper dish.

SERVES 4

30ml/2 tbsp vegetable oil
4 garlic cloves, crushed
4 shallots, finely chopped
30ml/2 tbsp yellow curry paste
2 kaffir lime leaves, torn
15ml/1 tbsp chopped fresh galangal
450g/1lb pumpkin, peeled, seeded and diced
225g/8oz sweet potatoes, diced
400ml/14fl oz/1²/₃ cups near-boiling vegetable stock
300ml/¹/₂ pint/1¹/₄ cups coconut milk
90g/3¹/₂oz/1¹/₂ cups chestnut mushrooms, sliced
15ml/1 tbsp soy sauce
90g/3¹/₂ oz/scant 1 cup peanuts, roasted and chopped
50g/2oz/¹/₃ cup pumpkin seeds, toasted, and fresh green chilli flowers, to garnish

1 Heat the oil in a frying pan. Add the garlic and shallots and cook over a medium heat, stirring occasionally, for 10 minutes, until softened and beginning to turn golden.

2 Add the yellow curry paste to the pan and stir-fry over a medium heat for 30 seconds, until fragrant. Transfer the mixture to the ceramic cooking pot.

3 Add the lime leaves, galangal, pumpkin and sweet potatoes to the cooking pot. Pour the stock and 150ml/¹/₄ pint/²/₃ cup of the coconut milk over the vegetables, and stir to combine. Cover with the lid and cook on high for 1¹/₂ hours.

4 Stir the mushrooms and soy sauce into the curry, then add the chopped peanuts and pour in the remaining coconut milk. Cover and cook on high for a further 3 hours, or until the vegetables are very tender.

5 Spoon the curry into warmed serving bowls, garnish with the pumpkin seeds and chilli flowers, and serve immediately.

Nutritional information per portion: Energy 337Kcal/1404kJ; Protein 10.3g; Carbohydrate 21.7g, of which sugars 10.8g; Fat 23.8g, of which saturates 4g; Cholesterol 0mg; Calcium 168mg; Fibre 5.1g; Sodium 554mg.

Potato, onion and garlic gratin

This tasty side dish makes the perfect accompaniment to vegetable casseroles and stews. Cooking the potatoes in stock with onions and garlic gives them a really rich flavour.

SERVES 4

40g/1¹/₂oz/3 tbsp butter
1 large onion, finely sliced into rings
2–4 garlic cloves, finely chopped
2.5ml/¹/₂ tsp dried thyme
900g/2lb waxy potatoes, very finely sliced
450ml/³/₄ pint/scant 2 cups boiling vegetable stock
salt and ground black pepper

1 Grease the inside of the cooking pot with 15g/¹/₂oz/1 tbsp of the butter. Spoon a thin layer of onions on to the base of the pot, then sprinkle over a little of the chopped garlic, dried thyme, salt and ground black pepper.

2 Arrange an overlapping layer of potato slices on top of the onion mixture. Layer the ingredients until all the onions, garlic, herbs and potatoes are used up, finishing with a layer of sliced potatoes.

3 Pour just enough of the stock into the pot to cover the potatoes. Cover and cook on low for 8–10 hours, or on high for 4–5 hours, until the potatoes are tender. Serve sprinkled with a little salt and ground black pepper.

Nutritional information per portion: Energy 260Kcal/1092kJ; Protein 5.1g; Carbohydrate 41.9g, of which sugars 6.4g; Fat 9.1g, of which saturates 5.4g; Cholesterol 21mg; Calcium 31mg; Fibre 3.3g; Sodium 171mg.

Orange candied sweet potatoes

Candied sweet potatoes are the classic accompaniment to a traditional Thanksgiving dinner. For a really fresh, festive look, serve with extra orange segments.

SERVES 8

900g/2lb sweet potatoes
150ml/¼ pint/²⁄₃ cup orange juice
30ml/2 tbsp maple syrup
5ml/1 tsp freshly grated ginger
2.5ml/½ tsp ground cinnamon
2.5ml/½ tsp ground cardamom
5ml/1 tsp salt
ground black pepper
orange segments, to serve (optional)

1 Peel the potatoes and cut them into 2cm/¾in cubes. Put them in a large heatproof bowl and pour over just enough boiling water to cover. Leave to stand for 5 minutes.

2 Meanwhile, put the orange juice, maple syrup, spices and salt in the ceramic cooking pot and stir to mix. Switch the slow cooker to high.

3 Drain the sweet potato cubes and add to the cooking pot. Gently stir to coat in the spicy orange mixture. Cover and cook for 4–5 hours, until tender, stirring twice during cooking.

4 Stir the orange segments, if using, into the sweet potatoes, and season to taste with pepper. Serve immediately.

Nutritional information per portion: Energy 53Kcal/226kJ; Protein 2.9g; Carbohydrate 13.7g, of which sugars 11.8g; Fat 0g, of which saturates 0g; Cholesterol 0mg; Calcium 5mg; Fibre 0.2g; Sodium 158mg.

Spiced Indian rice with spinach, tomatoes and cashew nuts

This all-in-one rice dish makes a delicious vegetarian meal but can also be served as an accompaniment to a meat curry. Ghee, the clarified butter used in much Indian cooking, is now widely available from large supermarkets as well as speciality food stores.

SERVES 4

30ml/2 tbsp sunflower oil

15ml/1 tbsp ghee or unsalted (sweet) butter

1 onion, finely chopped

2 garlic cloves, crushed

3 tomatoes, peeled, seeded and chopped

275g/10oz/1¹/₂ cups easy-cook (converted) brown rice

5ml/1 tsp each ground coriander and

ground cumin, or 10ml/2 tsp dhana jeera powder

2 carrots, coarsely grated

750ml/1¹/₄ pints/3 cups boiling vegetable stock

175g/6oz baby spinach leaves, washed

salt and ground black pepper

50g/2oz/¹/₂ cup unsalted cashew nuts, toasted, to garnish

1 Heat the oil and ghee or butter in a pan, add the onion and fry gently for 6–7 minutes, until soft. Add the garlic and tomatoes and cook for 2 minutes.

2 Rinse the rice in a sieve (strainer) under cold water, drain well and transfer to the pan. Add the coriander and cumin or dhana jeera powder and stir for a few seconds. Turn off the heat and transfer the mixture to the cooking pot.

3 Stir in the carrots, then pour in the stock, season with salt and pepper and stir to mix. Switch the slow cooker on to high. Cover and cook for 1 hour.

4 Lay the spinach on the surface of the rice, replace the lid and cook for a further 30–40 minutes, or until the spinach has wilted and the rice is cooked and tender.

5 Stir the spinach into the rice and check the seasoning, adding a little more salt and pepper if necessary. Sprinkle the cashew nuts over the rice and serve.

Nutritional information per portion: Energy 473Kcal/1989kJ; Protein 10.1g; Carbohydrate 72.1g, of which sugars 9.2g; Fat 18g, of which saturates 4.5g; Cholesterol 8mg; Calcium 111mg; Fibre 4.8g; Sodium 349mg.

Desserts and baking

From baked custards and poached fruit to

steamed puddings and luscious cakes,

this chapter is perfect for anyone with a

sweet tooth and a slow cooker. Try old-

fashioned favourites such as poached

pears, indulge yourself with a treat such

as chocolate chip and banana pudding or

enjoy a cup of tea or coffee with one of

the fabulous cakes.

Poached pears in red wine

The pears take on a red blush from the wine and make a very pretty dessert. This recipe works best in a small slow cooker, which ensures that the pears stay submerged during cooking.

SERVES 4

1 bottle fruity red wine
150g/5oz/¾ cup caster (superfine) sugar
45ml/3 tbsp clear honey
1 cinnamon stick
1 vanilla pod (bean), split length-ways
large strip of lemon or orange rind
2 whole cloves
2 black peppercorns
4 firm ripe pears
juice of ½ lemon
mint leaves, to garnish
whipped cream or sour cream, to serve

1 Pour the wine into the cooking pot. Add the sugar, honey, cinnamon stick, vanilla pod, lemon or orange rind, cloves and peppercorns. Cover and cook on high for 30 minutes, stirring occasionally.

2 Meanwhile, peel the pears, leaving the stem intact. Take a very thin slice off the base of each pear so it will stand square and upright. As each pear is peeled, toss it in the lemon juice to prevent it browning.

3 Place the pears in the spiced wine mixture in the pot. Cover and cook for 2–4 hours, turning occasionally, until they are just tender.

4 Transfer the pears to a bowl using a slotted spoon. Continue to cook the wine mixture uncovered for a further 1 hour, until the mixture is reduced and slightly thickened, then turn off the slow cooker and leave to cool.

5 Strain the cooled liquid over the pears and leave to chill in the refrigerator for at least 3 hours.

6 Place the pears in four serving dishes and spoon a little of the wine syrup over each one. Decorate with a few fresh mint leaves and serve with a spoonful of whipped or sour cream.

Nutritional information per portion: Energy 87Kcal/367kJ; Protein 0.5g; Carbohydrate 16.6g, of which sugars 16.6g; Fat 0.2g, of which saturates 0g; Cholesterol 0mg; Calcium 19mg; Fibre 3.3g; Sodium 7mg.

Winter fruit poached in mulled wine

Poaching fresh apples and pears with dried apricots and figs in a spicy wine syrup makes a delicious winter dessert. Serve on its own or with a generous spoonful of thick cream.

SERVES 4

300ml/¹/₂ pint/1¹/₄ cups fruity red wine

300ml/¹/₂ pint/1¹/₄ cups fresh apple or orange juice

thinly pared strip of orange or lemon peel

45ml/3 tbsp clear honey

1 small cinnamon stick

4 whole cloves

4 cardamom pods, split

2 pears, such as Comice or William

8 ready-to-eat figs

12 ready-to-eat dried unsulphured apricots

2 eating apples, peeled, cored and thickly sliced

1 Pour the wine and apple or orange juice into the ceramic cooking pot. Add the citrus peel, honey, cinnamon, cloves and cardamom pods. Cover with the lid and cook on high for 1 hour.

2 Peel, core and halve the pears, keeping the stalk intact if possible. Place in the cooker with the figs and apricots. Cook for 1 hour.

3 Gently turn the pears, then add the sliced apples and cook for a further 1¹/₂–2 hours, or until all the fruit is tender. Using a slotted spoon, remove the fruit from the pot and place in a serving dish. Set aside.

4 Strain the syrup into a pan, discarding the spices, then bring to the boil. Boil for 10 minutes. Pour over the fruit and serve hot or cold.

Nutritional information per portion: Energy 347Kcal/1476kJ; Protein 5g; Carbohydrate 78.1g, of which sugars 78.1g; Fat 1.9g, of which saturates 0g; Cholesterol 0mg; Calcium 284mg; Fibre 11.4g; Sodium 72mg.

Papaya cooked with ginger

Spicy ginger enhances the delicate flavour of papaya perfectly. This recipe is excellent for busy people because it takes no more than 10 minutes to prepare and can then be left to cook gently until it is ready to serve. Be careful not to overcook papaya or the flesh will become watery.

SERVES 4

150ml/¼ pint/⅔ cup hot water
45ml/3 tbsp raisins
shredded finely pared rind and
    juice of 1 lime
2 ripe papayas
2 pieces stem ginger in syrup,
    drained, plus 15ml/1 tbsp
    syrup from the jar

8 amaretti or other dessert biscuits
    (cookies), coarsely crushed
25g/1oz/¼ cup pistachio nuts,
    chopped
15ml/1 tbsp light muscovado
    (brown) sugar
60ml/4 tbsp crème fraîche, plus
    extra to serve

1 Pour the water into the base of the cooking pot and switch the slow cooker to high. Put the raisins in a small bowl and pour over the lime juice. Stir to combine, then leave to soak for at least 5 minutes, while preparing the remaining ingredients.

2 Cut the papayas in half and scoop out and discard their seeds, using a teaspoon.

3 Finely chop the stem ginger and combine with the biscuits, raisins and lime juice, lime rind, two-thirds of the nuts, the sugar and crème fraîche.

4 Fill the papayas with the mixture and place in the cooking pot. Cover and cook for 1–1½ hours. Drizzle with the ginger syrup, sprinkle with the remaining nuts and serve with crème fraîche.

VARIATION
Try using chopped almonds and Greek (strained plain) yogurt in place of the pistachio nuts and crème fraîche.

Nutritional information per portion: Energy 302Kcal/1272kJ; Protein 4.1g; Carbohydrate 45.6g, of which sugars 36.6g; Fat 12.8g, of which saturates 5.7g; Cholesterol 17mg; Calcium 70mg; Fibre 5.7g; Sodium 136mg.

Petits pots de crème au Mocha

The name of these French baked custards comes from the baking cups, which are called pots de crème. *The addition of coffee powder and coffee liqueur gives the dessert an even richer flavour.*

SERVES 4

5ml/1 tsp instant coffee powder
15ml/1 tbsp soft light brown sugar
300ml/¹/₂ pint/1¹/₄ cups milk
150ml/¹/₄ pint/²/₃ cup double (heavy) cream
115g/4oz plain (semisweet) chocolate
15ml/1 tbsp coffee liqueur (optional)
4 egg yolks
whipped cream and candied cake decorations, to decorate (optional)

1 Put the instant coffee and sugar in a pan and stir in the milk and cream. Bring to the boil over a medium heat, stirring constantly, until the coffee and sugar have dissolved completely.

2 Remove the pan from the heat and add the chocolate. Stir until the chocolate has melted, then stir in the coffee liqueur, if using.

3 In a bowl, whisk the egg yolks, then slowly whisk in the chocolate mixture until well blended. Strain the custard mixture into a large jug (pitcher) and divide equally among *pots de crème* or ramekins – first checking that they will all fit inside the cooking pot.

4 Cover each *pot de crème* or ramekin with a piece of foil, then transfer to the cooking pot. Pour enough hot water around the dishes to come just over halfway up their sides. Cover the slow cooker with the lid and cook on high for 2¹/₂–3 hours, or until they are just set and a knife inserted into the middle comes out clean.

5 Carefully remove the pots from the cooker and leave to cool. Cover and chill until ready to serve, then decorate with whipped cream and candied cake decorations, if you like.

Nutritional information per portion: Energy 443Kcal/1840kJ; Protein 8.3g; Carbohydrate 23.7g, of which sugars 23.7g; Fat 35.7g, of which saturates 20.2g; Cholesterol 264mg; Calcium 196mg; Fibre 0.2g; Sodium 74mg.

Chocolate chip and banana pudding

Rich, dense and sticky, this steamed pudding served with a glossy chocolate sauce is a great winter dessert. For an extra treat, serve with a scoop of vanilla ice cream.

SERVES 4

200g/7oz/1¾ cups self-raising (self-rising) flour

75g/3oz/6 tbsp unsalted (sweet) butter

2 ripe bananas, mashed

75g/3oz/6 tbsp caster (superfine) sugar

50ml/2fl oz/1¼ cups milk

1 egg, lightly beaten

75g/3oz/²/₃ cup chocolate chips

FOR THE CHOCOLATE SAUCE

90g/3½oz/½ cup caster (superfine) sugar

50ml/2fl oz/¼ cup water

175g/6oz/1¼ cups plain (semisweet) chocolate chips or chopped unsweetened chocolate

25g/1oz/2 tbsp unsalted (sweet) butter

30ml/2 tbsp brandy or orange juice

1 Grease and line the base of a 1 litre/1¾ pint/4 cup pudding basin. Put an inverted saucer into the cooking pot and pour in 2.5cm/1in hot water. Turn the cooker to high.

2 Sift the flour into a bowl and rub in the butter until the mixture resembles breadcrumbs. Stir in the bananas, then add the sugar and mix.

3 Whisk together the milk and egg in a small bowl, then beat into the banana mixture. Stir in the chocolate chips and spoon the mixture into the prepared basin.

4 Cover with a double thickness of buttered foil and place in the pot. Pour enough boiling water around the basin to come just over halfway up the sides. Cover and cook on high for 3–4 hours until the pudding is risen and a skewer inserted in the middle comes out clean. Turn off the cooker and leave in the water.

5 Heat the sugar and water in a pan until the sugar has dissolved. Remove from the heat, add the chocolate and stir until melted, then add the butter and stir. Stir in the brandy or juice. Serve with the sauce.

Nutritional information per portion: Energy 926Kcal/3890kJ; Protein 11.1g; Carbohydrate 131.9g, of which sugars 93.2g; Fat 41.1g, of which saturates 24.6g; Cholesterol 118mg; Calcium 266mg; Fibre 3.3g; Sodium 378mg.

Hot bananas with rum and raisins

These sticky, sweet baked bananas are utterly moreish and make a great dessert all year round. The rich sauce becomes almost toffee-like during cooking, and is irresistible.

SERVES 4

30ml/2 tbsp seedless raisins
45ml/3 tbsp dark rum
40g/1¹/₂oz/3 tbsp unsalted (sweet)
    butter, cut into cubes
50g/2oz/¹/₄ cup soft light brown sugar
4 slightly under-ripe bananas, peeled and
    halved lengthways
1.5ml/¹/₄ tsp grated nutmeg
1.5ml/¹/₄ tsp ground cinnamon
25g/1oz/¹/₄ cup flaked (sliced) almonds,
    toasted (optional), to decorate
whipped cream or vanilla ice cream,
    to serve

1 Put the raisins in a bowl and spoon over 30ml/2 tbsp of the rum. Leave to soak.

2 Place the butter in the cooking pot with the sugar and remaining rum. Switch the cooker to high and leave uncovered for 15 minutes, until the butter and sugar have melted. Add the bananas to the mixture, cover and cook for about 30 minutes, or until the fruit is almost tender, turning the bananas halfway through cooking.

3 Sprinkle the nutmeg and cinnamon over the bananas, then pour in the soaked raisins and rum remaining in the bowl. Stir very gently to mix well, then cover again and cook for a further 10 minutes.

4 Arrange the bananas on a serving dish or individual serving plates. Spoon over the sauce, then sprinkle with flaked almonds, if using. Serve the bananas hot with either whipped cream or vanilla ice cream.

Nutritional information per portion: Energy 323Kcal/1355kJ; Protein 3g; Carbohydrate 47.1g, of which sugars 44.7g; Fat 12.1g, of which saturates 5.6g; Cholesterol 21mg; Calcium 33mg; Fibre 1.9g; Sodium 72mg.

Sticky coffee and pear pudding

This dark and moist fruity pudding is complemented with a tangy citrus-flavoured cream. It is delicious served hot, but is equally good at room temperature.

SERVES 6

115g/4oz/¹/₂ cup butter, softened, plus extra for greasing
30ml/2 tbsp ground coffee
15ml/1 tbsp near-boiling water
4 small ripe pears
juice and finely grated rind of ¹/₂ orange
115g/4oz/generous ¹/₂ cup golden caster (superfine) sugar, plus 15ml/1 tbsp for baking
2 eggs, beaten

50g/2oz/¹/₂ cup self-raising (self-rising) flour, sifted
50g/2oz/¹/₂ cup toasted skinned hazelnuts, ground
45ml/3 tbsp maple syrup
fine strips of orange rind, to decorate

FOR THE ORANGE CREAM
300ml/¹/₂ pint/1¹/₄ cups whipping cream
15ml/1 tbsp icing (confectioners') sugar, sifted

1 Pour 2.5cm/1in hot water into the cooking pot. Place an upturned saucer in the base, then turn on to high. Grease and line the base of a deep 18cm/7in fixed-base cake tin (pan) or soufflé dish.

2 Put the coffee in a small bowl and pour the water over. Leave for 4 minutes, then strain through a fine sieve. Peel, halve and core the pears. Thinly slice across the pear halves part of the way through, then brush with the juice.

3 Beat the butter and the larger quantity of caster sugar together until light and fluffy. Gradually beat in the eggs. Fold the flour into the mixture. Add the hazelnuts and coffee. Spoon the mixture into the tin, and level the top.

4 Pat the pears dry on kitchen paper and arrange in a circle in the mixture, flat side down. Brush with some of the maple syrup, then sprinkle with 15ml/1 tbsp caster sugar. Cover with foil and place in the pot. Pour enough boiling water around the tin to come slightly more than halfway up the sides. Cover and cook for 3–3¹/₂ hours, until firm and well risen.

5 To make the orange cream, whip the cream, icing sugar and orange rind until soft peaks form. Chill. Let the sponge cool in the tin for 10 minutes, then turn on to a plate. Brush with the remaining maple syrup, then decorate with orange rind and serve with the orange cream.

Nutritional information per portion: Energy 852Kcal/3571kJ; Protein 12.5g; Carbohydrate 107g, of which sugars 45g; Fat 44.5g, of which saturates 23.8g; Cholesterol 169mg; Calcium 362mg; Fibre 5.3g; Sodium 493mg.

Steamed chocolate and fruit pudding

Drenched in a rich chocolate syrup, this wickedly indulgent steamed pudding makes a great alternative to a traditional Christmas pudding – although it is a fabulous treat at any time of year, the addition of cranberries gives it an unmistakably festive flavour.

SERVES 4

vegetable oil, for greasing
1 apple
25g/1oz/¼ cup cranberries, thawed if frozen
175g/6oz/¾ cup soft dark brown sugar
115g/4oz/½ cup soft margarine
2 eggs, lightly beaten
50g/2oz/½ cup self-raising (self-rising)
    flour, sifted
45ml/3 tbsp (unsweetened) cocoa powder

FOR THE SYRUP

115g/4oz plain (semisweet) chocolate,
    chopped
30ml/2 tbsp clear honey
15g/½oz/1 tbsp unsalted (sweet) butter
2.5ml/½ tsp vanilla extract

1 Pour 2.5cm/1in hot water into the cooking pot and switch the cooker to high. Oil four pudding basins and line with baking parchment.

2 Peel and core the apple, then dice the flesh. Place in a bowl, then add the cranberries and 15ml/1 tbsp of the sugar. Mix, then divide among the basins, patting it down into the base of each one.

3 Beat the remaining sugar, the margarine, eggs, flour and cocoa together until combined and smooth and creamy.

4 Spoon the mixture into the pudding basins and cover each with a double thickness of greased foil. Place the puddings in the cooking pot and pour in enough hot water to come about two-thirds up the sides. Cover and cook on high for 1½–2 hours until the puddings are risen and firm to the touch. Remove and leave to stand for 10 minutes.

5 Meanwhile, make the chocolate syrup. Put the chocolate, honey, butter and vanilla in a heatproof bowl and place in the hot water in the slow cooker. Leave for 10 minutes, until the butter has melted, then stir until smooth. Serve the puddings with the chocolate syrup.

Nutritional information per portion: Energy 739Kcal/3094kJ; Protein 9.1g; Carbohydrate 88.3g, of which sugars 77.2g; Fat 41.3g, of which saturates 14.4g; Cholesterol 124mg; Calcium 103mg; Fibre 3.1g; Sodium 438mg.

Fresh fruit bread and butter pudding

Fresh currants add a tart touch to this scrumptious hot pudding. For the best results, use a wide, shallow dish rather than a narrow, deep one, but make sure it fits comfortably in the slow cooker.

SERVES 4

40g/1½oz/3 tbsp butter, softened, plus
    extra for greasing
6 medium-thick slices of day-old bread,
    crusts removed
115g/4oz/1 cup prepared redcurrants
    and raspberries
3 eggs, beaten

50g/2oz/¼ cup golden caster
    (superfine) sugar
300ml/½ pint/1¼ cups creamy milk
5ml/1 tsp vanilla extract
freshly grated nutmeg
30ml/2 tbsp demerara sugar
single (light) cream, to serve

1 Butter a 1 litre/1¾ pints/4 cup round or oval baking dish – checking first that it fits in your slow cooker. Pour 2.5cm/1in of very hot water into the cooking pot. Place an upturned saucer in the base and switch the cooker to high.

2 Spread the slices of bread generously with the butter, then cut them in half diagonally. Arrange the bread triangles in the dish in neat layers, overlapping the slices, with the buttered side facing up. Scatter the fresh currants and berries over the bread and between the slices, ensuring that there is an even quantity of fruit throughout the pudding.

3 Place the eggs and caster sugar in a large bowl and beat together. Gradually whisk in the milk, vanilla and a large pinch of grated nutmeg until mixed.

4 Place the bread dish in the cooking pot, then pour the egg and milk mixture over the bread, pushing the bread slices down to submerge them. Scatter the demerara sugar and a little nutmeg over the top, then cover with foil.

5 Pour near-boiling water around the dish, so that the water level comes just over halfway up the sides of the dish. Cover and cook on high for 3–4 hours, or until a skewer inserted into the centre comes out clean.

6 Remove the dish from the cooker and, if you like, briefly brown the top of the pudding under a hot grill (broiler). Cool slightly, then serve with cream.

Nutritional information per portion: Energy 405Kcal/1700kJ; Protein 12.6g; Carbohydrate 53.7g, of which sugars 30.7g; Fat 16.9g, of which saturates 8.6g; Cholesterol 202mg; Calcium 234mg; Fibre 2.1g; Sodium 405mg.

Chocolate chip walnut cake

The tangy flavour of orange works well in this chocolate and nut loaf. It can be finished simply with a generous dusting of icing sugar, or as here with a zesty orange topping.

SERVES 8

115g/4oz/1 cup plain (all-purpose) flour
25g/1oz/¼ cup cornflour (cornstarch)
5ml/1 tsp baking powder
115g/4oz/½ cup butter, at room temperature
115g/4oz/½ cup golden caster (superfine) sugar
2 eggs, lightly beaten
75g/3oz/½ cup plain (semisweet), milk or white
   chocolate chips

50g/2oz/½ cup chopped walnuts
finely grated rind of ½ orange

FOR THE TOPPING
115g/4oz/1 cup icing (confectioners') sugar,
   sifted, plus 5ml/1 tsp for dusting
20–30ml/4 tsp–2 tbsp fresh orange juice
walnut halves, to decorate

1 Grease and line a 450g/1lb loaf tin (pan). Place an upturned saucer in the base of the cooking pot and pour in 2.5cm/1in very hot water. Switch the slow cooker to high.

2 Sift the flour, cornflour and baking powder together twice, so that the dry ingredients are well mixed and aerated, then set aside.

3 Place the butter in a large bowl and beat until creamy. Add the caster sugar and continue beating until light and fluffy. Add the eggs a little at a time, beating well after each addition. Gently fold about half of the sifted flour mixture into the creamed butter mixture, then add the rest with the chocolate chips, walnuts and orange rind. Fold in until just blended, taking care not to overmix.

4 Spoon the mixture into the loaf tin and loosely cover with a piece of foil, allowing some space at the top for the cake to rise as it cooks. Put the loaf tin in the cooking pot. Pour enough boiling water around the loaf tin to come two-thirds of the way up the sides. Cover and cook for 2½–3 hours, or until a skewer pushed into the centre of the cake comes out clean. Remove the cake and stand it on a wire rack for 10 minutes, then turn out and leave to cool on the rack.

5 To decorate, place 115g/4oz/1 cup icing sugar in a bowl. Stir in 20ml/4 tsp of the orange juice, adding a little more if needed to make the consistency of thick cream. Drizzle the mixture over the cake, then decorate with walnuts dusted with 5ml/1 tsp icing sugar. Leave to set before serving.

Nutritional information per portion: Energy 395Kcal/1655kJ; Protein 4.7g; Carbohydrate 51g, of which sugars 36.9g; Fat 20.5g, of which saturates 9.9g; Cholesterol 87mg; Calcium 49mg; Fibre 0.9g; Sodium 171mg.

Marbled spice cake

This cake can be baked in a fluted ring-shaped cake mould called a **kugelhupf** *or* **gugelhupf**, *which originates from Germany and Austria, or in a plain ring-shaped cake tin. The marbled effect looks particularly good when the cake is baked in a ring like this.*

SERVES 8

75g/3oz/6 tbsp butter, at room
    temperature, plus extra for greasing
115g/4oz/1/2 cup soft light brown sugar
2 eggs
few drops of vanilla extract
130g/41/2oz/generous 1 cup plain (all-
    purpose) flour, plus extra for dusting

7.5ml/11/2 tsp baking powder
45ml/3 tbsp milk
30ml/2 tbsp malt extract or black treacle
5ml/1 tsp mixed (apple pie) spice
2.5ml/1/2 tsp ground ginger
75g/3oz/3/4 cup icing (confectioners')
    sugar, sifted, to decorate

1 Grease and flour a 1.2 litre/2 pint/5 cup kugelhupf mould or ring-shaped cake tin (pan). Put an inverted saucer in the slow cooker and pour in 5cm/2in hot water. Switch the cooker to high.

2 Beat the butter and sugar together until light and fluffy. In another bowl, beat together the eggs and vanilla, then gradually beat into the butter mixture, adding a little at a time and beating after each addition.

3 Sift together the flour and baking powder, then fold into the butter mixture, adding a little milk between each addition. Spoon one-third of the mixture into a bowl and stir in the malt extract, spice and ginger.

4 Drop a large spoonful of the light mixture into the tin, followed by a spoonful of the dark mixture. Continue alternating spoonfuls of the light and dark mixtures until all the mixture has been used. Run a knife or skewer through the mixtures to give a marbled effect.

5 Cover with foil and place in the pot. Pour boiling water around the tin to come just over halfway up the sides. Cover and cook for 3–4 hours until a skewer inserted into the middle comes out clean. Remove and leave in the tin for 10 minutes before turning out on to a wire rack to cool.

6 Put the icing sugar in a bowl, add just enough warm water to create the consistency of single (light) cream and stir until smooth. Drizzle over the cake, then leave to set before serving.

Nutritional information per portion: Energy 215Kcal/902kJ; Protein 2.8g; Carbohydrate 33g, of which sugars 20.3g; Fat 8.8g, of which saturates 5.2g; Cholesterol 49mg; Calcium 84mg; Fibre 0.5g; Sodium 172mg.

Chocolate cheesecake brownies

A very dense chocolate brownie mixture is swirled with creamy cheese to give a marbled effect.
Cut into small squares for little mouthfuls of absolute heaven.

MAKES 9

50g/2oz dark (bittersweet) chocolate
   (minimum 70 per cent cocoa solids),
   chopped
50g/2oz/¼ cup unsalted (sweet) butter
65g/2¼oz/5 tbsp light muscovado
   (brown) sugar
1 egg, beaten
25g/1oz/¼ cup plain (all-purpose)
   flour, sifted

FOR THE CHEESECAKE MIXTURE

115g/4oz/½ cup full-fat cream cheese
25g/1oz/2 tbsp caster (superfine) sugar
5ml/1 tsp vanilla extract
½ beaten egg

1 Line a 15cm/6in square fixed-base cake tin (pan). Pour 5cm/2in hot water into the cooking pot and switch the slow cooker to high. Put the chocolate and butter in a heatproof bowl and place in the cooker. Leave for 10 minutes.

2 Beat the cheese, sugar and vanilla together. Gradually beat in the egg until smooth and creamy. Set aside. Stir the chocolate mixture until smooth, then remove from the cooker. Add the muscovado sugar and stir until combined.

3 Place an upturned saucer in the base of the cooking pot. Add the egg to the chocolate mixture a little at a time, and beat until mixed. Fold in the flour. Spoon the chocolate mixture into the base of the tin. Drop spoonfuls of the cheesecake mixture on top and swirl the mixtures together.

4 Cover with foil and place in the slow cooker. Pour in boiling water around the tin to come just over halfway up the sides. Cook for 2 hours until just set in the centre. Place the tin on a wire rack to cool.

Nutritional information per portion: Energy 174Kcal/727kJ; Protein 2.9g; Carbohydrate 16.2g, of which sugars 14g; Fat 11.3g, of which saturates 6.8g; Cholesterol 65mg; Calcium 25mg; Fibre 0.2g; Sodium 86mg.

Light fruit cake

This incredibly easy all-in-one fruit cake has a crumbly texture. The combination of wholemeal flour and long slow cooking ensures that it stays beautifully moist.

SERVES 12

2 eggs
130g/4¹/₂oz/generous ¹/₂ cup butter,
    at room temperature
225g/8oz/1 cup light muscovado (brown)
    sugar
150g/5oz/1¹/₄ cups self-raising
    (self-rising) flour
150g/5oz/1¹/₄ cups wholemeal (whole-
    wheat) self-raising (self-rising) flour
pinch of salt
5ml/1 tsp mixed (apple pie) spice
450g/1lb/2¹/₂ cups luxury mixed
    dried fruit

1 Line the base and sides of a deep 18cm/7in round or 15cm/6in square fixed-base cake tin (pan). Place an upturned saucer in the base of the cooking pot, then pour in 2.5cm/1in hot water. Switch the slow cooker to high.

2 Crack the eggs into a large bowl. Add the butter and sugar, then sift over the flours, salt and spice, adding any bran left in the sieve (strainer). Stir together until mixed, then add the dried fruit and beat for 2 minutes until the mixture is smooth and glossy.

3 Spoon the mixture into the cake tin and level the surface. Cover the tin with a piece of buttered foil. Put the tin in the slow cooker and pour in enough boiling water to come just over halfway up the sides of the tin. Cover and cook for 4–5 hours.

4 Place the cake on a wire rack and leave to cool in the tin for about 15 minutes, then turn out and leave to cool completely.

Nutritional information per portion: Energy 351Kcal/1482kJ; Protein 4.9g; Carbohydrate 63g, of which sugars 46g; Fat 10.6g, of which saturates 6g; Cholesterol 60.8mg; Calcium 78.6mg; Fibre 2.3g; Sodium 148mg.

Frosted carrot and parsnip cake

A delicious twist on the classic plain carrot cake, this version is wonderfully light and crumbly. Cooked meringue spread over the top makes a change from the usual cream cheese topping, and makes a stunning contrast to the wholesome, crumbly cake.

SERVES 8

oil, for greasing
1 orange or lemon
10ml/2 tsp caster (superfine) sugar
175g/6oz/³⁄₄ cup butter or margarine
175g/6oz/³⁄₄ cup soft light brown sugar
3 eggs, lightly beaten
175g/6oz carrots and parsnips, grated
50g/2oz/¹⁄₃ cup sultanas (golden raisins)
115g/4oz/1 cup self-raising (self-rising) flour

50g/2oz/¹⁄₂ cup self-raising
  (self-rising) wholemeal
  (whole-wheat) flour
5ml/1 tsp baking powder

FOR THE TOPPING
50g/2oz/¹⁄₄ cup caster (superfine) sugar
1 egg white
pinch of salt

1 Put an upturned saucer in the cooking pot and pour in 2.5cm/1in hot water. Turn the slow cooker to high. Oil a deep 18cm/7in round fixed-based cake tin (pan) or soufflé dish and line the base.

2 Grate the orange or lemon rind and put half in a bowl. Mix with the caster sugar, then arrange on greaseproof (waxed) paper and leave in a warm place to dry.

3 Beat the butter and brown sugar together until pale and fluffy. Add the eggs a little at a time, beating after each addition. Stir in the unsugared citrus rind, grated carrots and parsnips and sultanas. Sift the flours and baking powder together, then fold into the carrot mixture.

4 Transfer the mixture to the tin and level the top. Cover loosely with greased foil, then place in the pot. Pour enough boiling water around the tin to come just over halfway up the sides. Cover and cook for 3–5 hours, or until a skewer inserted in the centre of the cake comes out clean. Lift the tin out of the cooker and leave for 5 minutes. Turn the cake out on to a wire rack and leave until cool.

5 For the topping, place the sugar in a bowl over the near-simmering water in the cooker. Squeeze the juice from the orange and add 30ml/2 tbsp of the juice to the sugar. Stir until the sugar dissolves. Remove from the heat, add the egg white and salt, and whisk for 1 minute. Return to the heat and whisk for 6 minutes until stiff and glossy. Cool for 5 minutes, whisking frequently. Swirl the topping over the cake and leave for 1 hour to firm up. To serve, sprinkle with the sugared rind.

Nutritional information per portion: Energy 410Kcal/1718kJ; Protein 5.9g; Carbohydrate 53g, of which sugars 38.2g; Fat 20.8g, of which saturates 12.2g; Cholesterol 132mg; Calcium 98mg; Fibre 1.9g; Sodium 290mg.

Blueberry muffin pudding

You can't cook traditional muffins in a slow cooker but this delicious alternative will satisfy your cravings. It's especially good served barely warm with custard or crème fraîche.

SERVES 4

75g/3oz/6 tbsp butter, plus extra for
  greasing
75g/3oz/6 tbsp soft light brown sugar
105ml/7 tbsp buttermilk, at room
  temperature
2 eggs, lightly beaten, at room
  temperature
225g/8oz/2 cups self-raising
  (self-rising) flour
pinch of salt
5ml/1 tsp ground cinnamon
150g/5oz/1/4 cup fresh blueberries
10ml/2 tsp demerara (raw) sugar, for
  sprinkling
custard or crème fraîche, to serve

1 Place an upturned saucer in the slow cooker. Pour in 5cm/2in hot water, then switch the slow cooker to high. Grease a 1.5 litre/2 1/2 pint/ 6 1/4 cup heatproof dish – check first though that it will fit inside the slow cooker.

2 Put the butter and sugar in a heatproof jug (pitcher) and place in the cooking pot. Leave uncovered for 20 minutes, stirring, until melted, Remove and cool until tepid.

3 Stir in the buttermilk followed by the beaten egg until the mixture is well mixed.

4 Sift the flour, salt and cinnamon into a bowl. Stir in the blueberries, then make a hollow in the middle. Pour in the buttermilk mixture and quickly stir until just combined.

5 Spoon the mixture into the dish, then sprinkle the top with the demerara sugar. Cover with a piece of buttered foil and place in the cooking pot. Pour in a little more boiling water around the dish to come halfway up the sides.

6 Cover the slow cooker with the lid and cook for 3–4 hours, or until a skewer inserted in the middle comes out clean. Leave the pudding to cool slightly before serving with custard or crème fraîche.

COOK'S TIP
Because less liquid evaporates from the pudding in a slow cooker, the mixture is thicker than conventional muffin batter.

Nutritional information per portion: Energy 499Kcal/2101kJ; Protein 10.1g; Carbohydrate 76.2g, of which sugars 34.4g; Fat 19.2g, of which saturates 10.7g; Cholesterol 153mg; Calcium 262mg; Fibre 2.2g; Sodium 367mg.

Pumpkin and banana cake

Rather like a cross between a carrot cake and banana bread, this luscious cake is an excellent way of using some of the scooped-out pumpkin flesh after making Halloween lanterns.

SERVES 12

225g/8oz/2 cups self-raising
   (self-rising) flour
7.5ml/1½ tsp baking powder
2.5ml/½ tsp ground cinnamon
2.5ml/½ tsp ground ginger
pinch of salt
125g/5oz/10 tbsp soft light brown sugar
75g/3oz/¾ cup pecans or walnuts,
   chopped
115g/4oz pumpkin flesh, coarsely grated
2 small bananas, peeled and mashed
2 eggs, lightly beaten
150ml/¼ pint/⅔ cup sunflower oil

FOR THE TOPPING

50g/2oz/¼ cup butter
150g/5oz/⅔ cup soft cheese
1.5ml/¼ tsp vanilla extract
115g/4oz/1 cup icing (confectioners')
   sugar
pecan halves, to decorate

1 Line the base and sides of a deep 20cm/8in round fixed-base cake tin (pan) or soufflé dish. Place an upturned saucer in the base of the cooking pot, then pour in about 2.5cm/1in hot water. Switch the slow cooker to high.

2 Sift the flour, baking powder, cinnamon, ginger and salt into a bowl to combine. Stir in the sugar, nuts and pumpkin until mixed. Make a hollow in the middle.

3 In a separate bowl, combine the bananas, eggs and oil, then stir into the dry ingredients. Turn into the tin and level the top. Cover the tin with buttered foil and place in the slow cooker. Pour in enough boiling water to come just over halfway up the sides of the tin.

4 Cover and cook on high for 4–4½ hours, or until the cake is firm and a skewer inserted into the middle comes out clean. Stand the tin on a wire rack to cool for 15 minutes. Turn out and leave until cold, then peel off the lining paper.

5 For the topping, put the butter, cheese and vanilla in a bowl and beat until smooth. Sift in the icing sugar and beat until smooth. Spread the topping over the top of the cake and decorate with pecans. Chill for at least 1 hour before serving.

Nutritional information per portion: Energy 374Kcal/1567kJ; Protein 5.1g; Carbohydrate 43.2g, of which sugars 28.7g; Fat 21.3g, of which saturates 6.5g; Cholesterol 58mg; Calcium 101.7mg; Fibre 1g; Sodium 203mg.

Moist golden ginger cake

This is the ultimate ginger cake: instead of black treacle, a mixture of golden syrup and malt extract gives a really sticky texture. Because of the long cooking, the cake matures sufficiently to eat straight away. However, the flavour improves if it is wrapped and kept for a day or two.

SERVES 10

175g/6oz/generous ³/4 cup light muscovado
  (brown) sugar
115g/4oz/¹/2 cup butter
150g/5oz/²/3 cup golden (light corn) syrup
25g/1oz malt extract
175g/6oz/1¹/2 cups self-raising (self-rising) flour

50g/2oz/¹/2 cup plain (all-purpose) flour
10ml/2 tsp ground ginger
pinch of salt
1 egg, lightly beaten
120ml/4fl oz/¹/2 cup milk, at room temperature
2.5ml/¹/2 tsp bicarbonate of soda (baking soda)

1 Line the base of a deep 18cm/7in round fixed-base cake tin (pan) or soufflé dish. Pour 5cm/2in hot water into the cooking pot. Switch the slow cooker to high.

2 Place the sugar, butter, golden syrup and malt extract in a heatproof bowl that will fit inside the slow cooker. Place in the cooking pot and leave for 15 minutes until melted.

3 Remove from the slow cooker and stir until smooth. Place an upturned saucer in the base of the cooking pot.

4 Sift the flours, ginger and salt into a separate bowl. Pour the melted butter and sugar mixture into the flour and beat until smooth. Stir in the beaten egg until well mixed.

5 Pour the milk in a jug (pitcher) and stir in the bicarbonate of soda. Pour the mixture into the ginger cake mixture and stir until combined.

6 Pour the cake mixture into the tin, cover with foil and place in the cooking pot. Pour a little more boiling water around the tin to come just over halfway up the sides. Cover and cook for 5–6 hours, or until firm and a skewer inserted into the middle of the cake comes out clean.

7 Remove the cake from the cooker and place the tin on a wire cooling rack. Leave to cool for 15 minutes, then turn out and leave to cool completely before serving in slices.

Nutritional information per portion: Energy 289Kcal/1216kJ; Protein 3.4g; Carbohydrate 48g, of which sugars 31.1g; Fat 10.6g, of which saturates 6.4g; Cholesterol 48mg; Calcium 98mg; Fibre 0.7g; Sodium 211mg.

Preserves and drinks

Although the slow cooker isn't suitable for jams, jellies and marmalades, it is perfect for making rich chutneys and relishes. The long, slow cooking develops flavours to such an extent that long maturation is unnecessary, so many relishes can be eaten immediately. You will also find a number of delicious drinks here.

Butternut, apricot and almond chutney

Coriander seeds and turmeric add a slightly spicy touch to this rich golden chutney. It is delicious spooned on to little savoury canapés or with melting cubes of mozzarella cheese; it is also good in sandwiches – helping to spice up bland or run-of-the-mill fillings.

MAKES ABOUT 1.8KG/4LB

1 small butternut squash, weighing about
   800g/1³/₄ lb
400g/14oz/2 cups golden
   granulated sugar
300ml/¹/₂ pint/1¹/₄ cups cider vinegar
2 onions, finely chopped
225g/8oz/1 cup ready-to-eat dried
   apricots, chopped
finely grated rind and juice of 1 orange
2.5ml/¹/₂ tsp turmeric
15ml/1 tbsp coriander seeds
15ml/1 tbsp salt
115g/4oz/1 cup flaked (sliced) almonds

1 Halve the butternut squash and scoop out the seeds. Peel off the skin, then cut the flesh into 1cm/¹/₂in cubes.

2 Put the sugar and vinegar in the cooking pot and switch to high. Heat for 30 minutes, then stir until the sugar has dissolved.

3 Add the butternut squash, onions, apricots, orange rind and juice, turmeric, coriander seeds and salt to the slow cooker and stir well.

4 Cover and cook for 5–6 hours, stirring occasionally. After 5 hours the chutney should be a fairly thick consistency with relatively little liquid. If it is still quite runny at this stage, cook uncovered for the final hour. Stir in the flaked almonds.

5 Spoon the chutney into warmed sterilized jars, cover and seal. Store in a cool, dark place and allow to mature for at least 1 month before eating. Use within 2 years. Once opened, store the chutney in the refrigerator and use within 2 months.

Nutritional information (total): Energy 2770Kcal/11723kJ; Protein 41.7g; Carbohydrate 532.6g, of which sugars 524.1g; Fat 67.3g, of which saturates 5.9g; Cholesterol 0mg; Calcium 807mg; Fibre 31.6g; Sodium 5967mg.

Mango chutney

No Indian meal would be complete without this classic chutney. Its gloriously sweet, tangy flavour complements the warm taste of spices perfectly. It is also great served with chargrilled chicken or duck breasts, and will liven up cheese sandwiches a treat.

MAKES 450G/1LB

3 firm mangoes
120ml/4fl oz/¹/₂ cup cider vinegar
200g/7oz/scant 1 cup light muscovado
   (brown) sugar
1 small red finger chilli or jalapeño
   chilli, split
2.5cm/1in piece of fresh root ginger,
   peeled and finely chopped
1 garlic clove, finely chopped
5 cardamom pods, bruised
1 bay leaf
2.5ml/¹/₂ tsp salt

1 Peel the mangoes and cut out the stone, then cut the flesh into small chunks or thin wedges.

2 Put the chopped mango in the ceramic cooking pot. Add the cider vinegar, stir briefly to combine, and cover the slow cooker with the lid.

Switch to high and cook for about 2 hours, stirring the chutney halfway through the cooking time.

3 Stir the sugar, chilli, ginger, garlic, bruised cardamoms, bay leaf and salt into the mango mixture until the sugar has dissolved completely.

4 Cover and cook for 2 hours, then uncover and cook for a further 1 hour, or until the chutney is reduced to a thick consistency and no excess liquid remains. Stir the chutney every 15 minutes during the last hour.

5 Remove and discard the bay leaf and the chilli. Spoon the chutney into hot sterilized jars and seal. Store for 1 week before eating and use within 1 year.

COOK'S TIP
To make a more fiery chutney, seed and slice two green chillies and stir into the chutney mixture with the other spices.

Nutritional information (total): Energy 1045Kcal/4465kJ; Protein 4.1g; Carbohydrate 272.5g, of which sugars 271.1g; Fat 0.9g, of which saturates 0.5g; Cholesterol 0mg; Calcium 908mg; Fibre 11.7g; Sodium 1002mg.

Beetroot, date and orange preserve

With its vibrant red colour and rich earthy flavour, this distinctive chutney is good with salads as well as full-flavoured cheeses such as mature Cheddar, Stilton or Gorgonzola.

MAKES ABOUT 1.4KG/3LB

300ml/¹/₂ pint/1¹/₄ cups malt vinegar
200g/7oz/1 cup granulated sugar
350g/12oz raw beetroot (beets)
350g/12oz eating apples
225g/8oz red onions, very finely chopped
1 garlic clove, crushed
finely grated rind of 2 oranges
5ml/1 tsp ground allspice
5ml/1 tsp salt
175g/6oz/1 cup chopped dried dates

1 Put the vinegar and sugar in the cooking pot. Cover and switch the slow cooker to high. Leave until steaming hot.

2 Meanwhile, scrub or thinly peel the beetroot, then cut into 1cm/¹/₂in pieces. Peel, quarter and core the apples and cut into 1cm/¹/₂in pieces.

3 Stir the vinegar mixture until the sugar has dissolved. Add the beetroot, apples, onions, garlic, orange rind, ground allspice and salt. Stir together, then re-cover and cook for 4–5 hours, stirring occasionally until very tender.

4 Stir in the dates and cook for a further hour until the mixture is really thick. Stir occasionally to prevent the chutney catching on the base of the pot.

5 Spoon the chutney into warmed sterilized jars, cover and seal. Store in a cool, dark place and open within 5 months of making. Chill after opening and use within 1 month.

Nutritional information (total): Energy 1632Kcal/6949kJ; Protein 16.8g; Carbohydrate 413.7g, of which sugars 406g; Fat 1.5g, of which saturates 0.2g; Cholesterol 0mg; Calcium 278mg; Fibre 23.1g; Sodium 2241mg.

Papaya and lemon relish

This chunky relish is best made with a firm, unripe papaya. The slow, gentle cooking allows all the flavours to mellow. Serve with roast meats, or with cheese and crackers.

MAKES 450G/1LB

1 large unripe papaya
1 onion, very thinly sliced
175ml/6fl oz/generous ³/₄ cup red
    wine vinegar
juice of 2 lemons
165g/5¹/₂oz/³/₄ cup golden caster
    (superfine) sugar
1 cinnamon stick
1 bay leaf
2.5ml/¹/₂ tsp hot paprika
2.5ml/¹/₂ tsp salt
150g/5oz/1 cup sultanas (golden raisins)

1 Peel the papaya and cut it lengthways in half. Remove the seeds, then cut the flesh into small chunks.

2 Place the papaya in the cooking pot, add the onion slices and stir in the vinegar. Switch the slow cooker to high, cover and cook for 2 hours.

3 Add the lemon juice, sugar, cinnamon stick, bay leaf, paprika, salt and sultanas, and stir until the sugar has completely dissolved.

4 Cook the chutney, uncovered, for a further 1 hour to allow the mixture to reduce slightly; the relish should be fairly thick and syrupy.

5 Ladle the chutney into hot sterilized jars. Seal and store for 1 week before using. Open within 1 year of making. Once opened, store in the refrigerator and use within 2 weeks.

Nutritional information (total): Energy 1294Kcal/5511kJ; Protein 8.4g; Carbohydrate 332.7g, of which sugars 332.7g; Fat 1.4g, of which saturates 0g; Cholesterol 0mg; Calcium 272mg; Fibre 16.1g; Sodium 1111mg.

Sweet and hot dried-fruit chutney

This rich, thick and slightly sticky preserve of spiced dried fruit is a wonderful way to enliven cold roast turkey left over from Christmas or Thanksgiving dinner.

MAKES ABOUT 1.5KG/3LB 6OZ

350g/12oz/1¹/₂ cups ready-to-eat dried apricots

225g/8oz/1¹/₂ cups dried dates, stoned (pitted)

225g/8oz/1¹/₃ cups dried figs

50g/2oz/¹/₃ cup glacé (candied) citrus peel

150g/5oz/1 cup raisins

50g/2oz/¹/₂ cup dried cranberries

75ml/2¹/₂fl oz/¹/₃ cup cranberry juice

300ml/¹/₂ pint/1¹/₄ cups cider vinegar

225g/8oz/1 cup caster (superfine) sugar

finely grated rind of 1 lemon

5ml/1 tsp mixed (apple pie) spice

5ml/1 tsp ground coriander

5ml/1 tsp cayenne pepper

5ml/1 tsp salt

1 Roughly chop the apricots, dates, figs and citrus peel, then put all the dried fruit in the cooking pot. Pour over the cranberry juice, stir, then cover with the lid and switch the slow cooker on to low. Cook for 1 hour, or until the fruit has absorbed most of the juice.

2 Add the cider vinegar and sugar to the fruit mixture. Turn the slow cooker up to the high setting and stir until the sugar has dissolved.

3 Cover and cook for a further 2 hours, or until the fruit is very soft and the chutney fairly thick (it will thicken further as it cools). Stir in the lemon rind, mixed spice, coriander, cayenne pepper and salt. Cook uncovered for 30 minutes, until little excess liquid remains.

4 Spoon the chutney into warmed sterilized jars, cover and seal. Store in a cool, dark place. Open within 10 months of making. Once opened, store in the refrigerator and use within 2 months.

Nutritional information (total): Energy 2873Kcal/12248kJ; Protein 32g; Carbohydrate 714.3g, of which sugars 703.5g; Fat 6.8g, of which saturates 0.2g; Cholesterol 0mg; Calcium 1075mg; Fibre 52.1g; Sodium 2358mg.

Fresh lemon curd

This classic tangy, creamy curd is still one of the most popular of all the curds. Delicious spread thickly over freshly baked white bread or served with American-style pancakes, it also makes a wonderfully rich, zesty sauce spooned over fresh fruit tarts.

MAKES ABOUT 450G/1LB

finely grated rind and juice of 3 lemons
   (preferably unwaxed or organic)
200g/7oz/1 cup caster (superfine) sugar
115g/4oz/1/2 cup unsalted (sweet)
   butter, diced
2 large (US extra large) eggs
2 large (US extra large) egg yolks

1 Pour 5cm/2in hot water into the cooking pot and switch the slow cooker to high. Put the lemon rind and juice, sugar and butter in the largest heatproof bowl that will fit inside the slow cooker.

2 Put the bowl into the cooker, then pour enough near-boiling water around it to come just over halfway up the sides. Leave for 15 minutes, stirring occasionally, until the sugar has dissolved and the butter melted. Leave to cool for a few minutes. Turn the slow cooker to low.

3 Put the eggs and yolks in a bowl and beat together with a fork. Strain the eggs into the lemon mixture, and whisk until combined. Cover with foil, then return to the cooker.

4 Cook on low for 1–2 hours, stirring every 15 minutes, until thick enough to coat the back of a wooden spoon.

5 Pour the lemon curd into small warmed sterilized jars. Cover and seal tightly.

6 Store the curd in a cool, dark place, ideally in the refrigerator, and use within 3 months. Once it is opened, store in the refrigerator and use within 1 month.

Nutritional information (total): Energy 1968Kcal/8224kJ; Protein 22.4g; Carbohydrate 215.3g, of which sugars 215.3g; Fat 118.9g, of which saturates 66.9g; Cholesterol 1102mg; Calcium 277mg; Fibre 0g; Sodium 895mg.

Hot spiced wine

The slow cooker is useful when you are making this wine for guests: you can prepare the wine up to four hours in advance, and the cooker will keep it hot until you are ready to serve.

SERVES 8

50g/2oz/¼ cup soft light brown sugar
150ml/¼ pint/⅔ cup near-boiling water
2 small oranges, preferably unwaxed
6 whole cloves
1 stick cinnamon
½ whole nutmeg
1½ bottles red wine, such as Bordeaux
150ml/¼ pint/⅔ cup brandy

1 Put the sugar in the cooking pot and pour in the near-boiling water. Stir until the sugar has dissolved, then switch the slow cooker to high.

2 Rinse the oranges, then press the cloves into one and add it to the slow cooker with the cinnamon, nutmeg and wine. Halve the remaining orange, then slice and set aside. Cover and cook on high or auto for 1 hour, then reduce to low or leave on auto and heat for 3 hours.

3 Stir the brandy into the spiced wine and add the orange slices. Heat for a further 1 hour.

4 Remove the whole orange and the cinnamon stick. The wine is now ready to serve and can be kept hot for up to 4 hours. Serve in heatproof glasses.

Nutritional information per portion: Energy 162Kcal/675kJ; Protein 0.2g; Carbohydrate 6.8g, of which sugars 6.8g; Fat 0g, of which saturates 0g; Cholesterol 0mg; Calcium 12mg; Fibre 0g; Sodium 10mg.

Cranberry and apple punch

When you are throwing a party, it is good to have a non-alcoholic punch available. Here, the slow cooker extracts maximum flavour from fresh ginger and lime peel.

SERVES 6

1 lime
5cm/2in piece of fresh root ginger, peeled and thinly sliced
50g/2oz/¼ cup caster (superfine) sugar
200ml/7fl oz/scant 1 cup near-boiling water
475ml/16fl oz/2 cups cranberry juice
475ml/16fl oz/2 cups clear apple juice
ice and chilled sparkling mineral water or soda water, to serve (optional)

1 Pare the rind off the lime and place in the cooking pot with the ginger and sugar. Pour over the water and stir until the sugar dissolves. Cover and heat on high or auto for 1 hour, then reduce the temperature to low or leave on auto and heat for a further 2 hours. Switch off the slow cooker and leave to cool completely.

2 When cold, strain the syrup through a sieve (strainer) into a large jug (pitcher) or punch bowl and discard the lime rind and ginger. Squeeze the juice from the lime and strain through a sieve into the syrup. Stir in the cranberry and apple juices. Cover and chill for at least 3 hours.

3 To serve, pour or ladle the punch over plenty of ice in tall glasses and top up with sparkling mineral water or soda water, if using.

Nutritional information per portion: Energy 111Kcal/475kJ; Protein 0.1g; Carbohydrate 27.9g, of which sugars 16.5g; Fat 0.1g, of which saturates 0g; Cholesterol 0mg; Calcium 8mg; Fibre 0g; Sodium 2mg.

Normandy coffee

The Normandy region of France is known for its orchards, and its name is given to dishes made with them. This recipe combines the flavour of apples and spices to make a delicious coffee.

SERVES 4

475ml/16fl oz/2 cups apple juice
30ml/2 tbsp soft brown sugar, to taste
2 oranges, thickly sliced
2 small cinnamon sticks
2 whole cloves
pinch of ground allspice
475ml/16fl oz/2 cups hot, freshly brewed strong black coffee
halved cinnamon sticks, to serve (optional)

1 Pour the apple juice into the cooking pot and switch the slow cooker on to high.

2 Add the sugar, oranges, cinnamon sticks, cloves and allspice to the pot and stir. Cover and heat for 20 minutes.

3 Stir the mixture until the sugar has dissolved completely, then cover with the lid and heat for 1 hour.

4 When the juice is hot and infused with the spices, switch the slow cooker to low to keep warm for up to 2 hours.

5 Strain the juice into a bowl, discarding the orange slices and spices. Pour the hot coffee into the juice and stir. Quickly pour into warmed mugs or espresso-style cups, adding a halved cinnamon stick to each, if you like.

Nutritional information per portion: Energy 85Kcal/363kJ; Protein 0.2g; Carbohydrate 22.2g, of which sugars 22.2g; Fat 0.1g, of which saturates 0g; Cholesterol 0mg; Calcium 11mg; Fibre 0g; Sodium 3mg.

Mexican hot chocolate

Blending the chocolate before serving gives it a frothy texture. The slow cooker is good because the gentle heating allows the spices to infuse the hot chocolate with a warm flavour.

SERVES 4

1 litre/1¾ pints/4 cups milk
1 cinnamon stick
2 whole cloves
115g/4oz dark (bittersweet) chocolate, chopped into
    small pieces
2–3 drops of almond extract
whipped cream and cocoa powder or grated chocolate,
    to serve (optional)

1 Pour the milk into the cooking pot. Add the cinnamon stick and cloves, cover with the lid and switch the slow cooker to high. Leave to heat the milk and infuse the spices for 1 hour, or until the milk is almost boiling.

2 Add the chocolate pieces and almond extract to the milk and stir until melted. Turn off the slow cooker.

3 Strain the mixture into a blender (it may be necessary to do this in two batches) and whizz on high speed for about 30 seconds, until frothy. Alternatively, whisk the mixture in the cooking pot with a hand-held electric whisk or a wire whisk.

4 Pour or ladle the hot chocolate into warmed heatproof glasses. If you like, top each with a little whipped cream and a dusting of cocoa powder or grated chocolate. Serve immediately.

Nutritional information per portion: Energy 262Kcal/1102kJ; Protein 9.9g; Carbohydrate 30g, of which sugars 29.7g; Fat 12.3g, of which saturates 7.6g; Cholesterol 17mg; Calcium 309mg; Fibre 0.7g; Sodium 109mg.

Slow cooker basics

This section shows you how to use

your slow cooker to its full potential

and provides tips on looking after it.

You will also discover which ingredients

are suitable and how to prepare them,

how to make stocks, sweet sauces,

savoury sauces, stews and casseroles,

and how to use your cooker safely.

Getting started

The basic principle behind the slow cooker is that it cooks food very slowly at a low temperature. The heat gradually builds up and is then maintained at an even level throughout the cooking time, to give perfect, tender results. Slow cookers are extremely simple and economical to use. They have a low wattage that consumes about the same amount of electricity as an ordinary light bulb, which makes them environmentally friendly.

Choosing a slow cooker

There is a wide selection of slow cookers available. They come in a range of sizes, shapes, colours and prices, and it is these factors that you will need to think about before you decide which type of slow cooker is right for you.

When slow cookers were first manufactured, the earthenware or ceramic pots were permanently fixed into the heat-resistant plastic or aluminium outer casing. While it is still possible to buy models made this way, most modern versions have a removable cooking pot that fits snugly into an inner metal casing. This newer style not only simplifies washing up, but allows the cooking pot to be lifted out and taken to the table as a serving dish.

Slow cookers may be round or oval in shape. Round versions are extremely good for cooking casseroles, steaming desserts and cooking cakes in round tins (pans), while oval slow cookers are better for pot-roasted meats and for use with loaf tins (pans) and terrines.

The size of different slow cookers can vary enormously – from a small 600ml/1 pint/2½ cup cooking pot to a 6.5 litre/11¼ pint/26¼ cup one.

BELOW: *Oval-shaped slow cookers are perfect for cooking certain types of food, such as pot-roasted joints of meat, long, loaf-shaped terrines, and small whole fish.*

Guide to cooking times

You can often introduce some flexibility to the total cooking time by adjusting the temperature setting. Certain foods are only successful if cooked at the specified setting. Cakes, for example, should always be cooked on high for the entire cooking time, and pot-roasted meats and egg-based recipes should usually be started on high (or auto) for the first hour of cooking, and then reduced. For dishes such as soups and casseroles, the cooking time may be shortened or extended to suit your needs by cooking on a higher or lower setting. As a rough guide, the cooking time on high is just over half that on low.

Low	Medium	High
6–8 hours	4–6 hours	3–4 hours
8–10 hours	6–8 hours	5–6 hours
10–12 hours	8–10 hours	7–8 hours

Of all the sizes, the most popular size is probably 3.5 litres/6 pints/14¼ cups, which will enable you to cook a wide range of dishes and cater easily for four people.

Preheating

Some slow cookers need to be preheated on high for 15–20 minutes before cooking. However, always check the instructions first. To preheat the slow cooker, place the empty cooking pot and lid in the slow cooker base and switch the temperature on to the high setting.

Slow cooker care

Wash the ceramic cooking pot well in hot soapy water, rinse and dry thoroughly. After use, the slow cooker should be switched off before removing the ceramic cooking pot. If you don't want to wash the pot immediately, it can be filled with warm water and left to soak for as long as necessary. However, do not immerse the entire pot in water for long periods of time because the base is usually porous and soaking may damage the pot. Very few cooking pots are dishwasher-proof.

Never plunge the hot cooking pot into cold water immediately after use, or pour boiling water into an empty cold cooking pot. Subjecting it to a sudden change in temperature could cause it to crack. Never immerse the outer casing in water or fill it with water. Always use a damp soapy cloth to clean it. During cooking, the pot and lid will become hot, so always use oven gloves when handling.

BELOW: *Smaller slow cookers intended for cooking just one or two portions at a time are a tremendous asset for single people and couples.*

Tips for success

During cooking, steam will condense on the lid of the slow cooker, then slowly trickle back into the pot. This helps to form a seal around the lid, retaining heat, flavour and cooking smells. If possible, avoid lifting the lid during cooking because this will cause heat loss. Should you need to lift the lid though, add an extra 15–20 minutes to the cooking time to make up for the heat lost. There is no need to stir food frequently because slow cooking prevents the food from sticking or bubbling over.

If at the end of the cooking time the food is not quite ready, replace the lid and switch the slow cooker to high to speed up the cooking process. Once ready, many dishes can be kept hot for an hour or so without risk of spoiling, by switching the slow cooker to low.

Tips on cooking: beef

Enjoyed all over the world, there are dozens of classic beef dishes, from the British Sunday roast, to French boeuf bourguignonne. Beef's popularity is partly due to its versatility. There are many different cuts of beef, and many of these are suitable for a range of cooking methods. Shin of beef, for example, is unsuitable for roasting but is great in stews and perfect for the slow cooker.

Buying and storing

As with all meat, the flavour and texture of beef is determined by the breed of the animal, its feed, the environment in which it is reared and, ultimately, by the process of slaughtering and the treatment of meat before it is cooked. While pork, veal and lamb tend to come from very young animals, beef usually comes from those aged between 18 months and 2 years.

Beef should be kept on a low shelf in the refrigerator, below any cooked foods and ingredients that will be eaten raw. When buying pre-packed meat, check and observe the eat-by date. Whether pre-packed or loose, minced (ground) and cubed beef should be used within 1–2 days of buying; chops and small joints should be used within 3 days, and larger joints within 4–5 days.

CUTS OF BEEF

Blade or chuck These cuts come from the top forequarter and are usually boned and sold together as braising steak. They suit pot-roasting, casseroling and braising.

Brisket This may be bought on the bone or boned and rolled and comes from the lower part of the shoulder. It is excellent pot-roasted, braised or stewed.

Clod and neck These cuts come from the neck and are fairly lean. They are often sold cut up as "stewing" steak and may also be sold minced (ground).

Fillet/tenderloin, rump/round, sirloin steak These lean cuts from the back may be included in braised slow cooker recipes, but are not suitable in casseroles and similar long-cooked dishes.

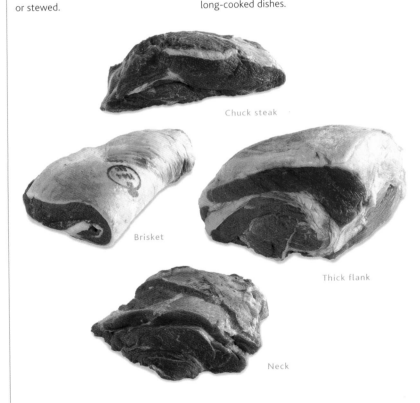

Chuck steak

Brisket

Thick flank

Neck

ABOVE: *Chuck steak and brisket are tough cuts, but both have an excellent flavour. They are suited to stewing, which gives delicious results. Thick flank is lean and it makes good braising steak. Neck is one of the less tender beef cuts but is delicious braised or stewed.*

Flank Lean thick flank, or top rump, comes from the hindquarter of the animal. In a whole piece, it is perfect for pot-roasting.

Leg and shin/foreshank The leg cut comes from the hind legs and the shin from the forelegs. The shin responds well to slow cooking.

Minced/ground beef This can be used to make meatballs. Darker meat has less fat than paler meat.

Rib Fore rib and wing, or prime rib, are expensive joints, and they are best served roasted. For use in the slow cooker, choose middle rib.

Silverside/round pot roast This is excellent for pot-roasts and braised dishes.

Skirt/flank steak This thin braising cut can also be pot-roasted. It has a lean but somewhat coarse texture, so is an ideal cut for the slow cooker.

VEAL

This meat comes from young calves, usually between 1 and 3 months in age, so it is very tender and lean. Most cuts are not well suited to cooking in the slow cooker. Exceptions are shoulder of veal, which is sometimes cut into chunks for casseroles; and the knuckle, the bonier end of the hind leg, which can be cut into slices and used to make the Italian *osso bucco*.

Thin flank

Skirt

Onglet

Topside

Knuckle

Shoulder

ABOVE: *Thin flank is best suited to slow, moist methods of cooking. Skirt and onglet are lean cuts with a coarse texture that become moist and tender when slowly braised. Topside is a fairly lean cut of beef that is best slowly braised or pot-roasted.*

ABOVE: *Veal's comparatively high water content makes it unsuitable in general for cooking for a long period of time. Knuckle and shoulder (also known as the oyster) are two of the few cuts of veal suitable for slow-cooker cooking.*

Lamb

Though lamb cuts do not usually need tenderizing, the fragrant flavour of the meat is intensified by slow cooking. It is enjoyed around the world in a wealth of pot-roasts, casseroles, stews, tagines, curries and braised dishes.

Buying and storing

Lamb comes from animals that are less than a year old; spring lamb comes from animals that are between five and seven months old. Meat from older sheep is known as mutton and has a darker colour and stronger flavour; it is rarely available. Look for firm, slightly pink lamb with a fine-grained texture. The fat should be creamy white, firm and waxy. Avoid meat that looks dark, dry or grainy or that has yellowing fat.

Lamb should be kept covered on a low shelf in the refrigerator. Pre-packed meat can be left in its packaging and used by the date given on the packet. When buying loose meat from the butcher, steaks and chops will keep for 2–3 days, while larger joints will keep for up to 5 days. If you wish to keep lamb for longer, freeze it in freezer bags and use within 3–4 months for minced (ground) lamb and 6–9 months for chops.

CUTS OF LAMB

The lean, tender prime cuts are taken from the top of the lamb along the middle of the back and are often grilled (broiled), fried or roasted. However, they may also be cooked using slow, moist methods. Tougher cuts from the neck and lower legs respond well to slow cooking.

Breast This inexpensive cut is fairly fatty and often served boned and rolled. It can be braised in the slow cooker, but trim off the visible fat.

Chops and cutlets Chump or loin chops and leg chops are thick tender chops. Best-end chops or cutlets and middle neck cutlets are thinner and should be trimmed of fat before slow cooking.

Leg This is the prime roasting joint and is often divided into two pieces: the knuckle or shank end, and the leg fillet. The shank is good pot-roasted or gently braised. A small leg may be pot-roasted on the bone, or it can be boned and stuffed. It may also be cut into leg steaks or cubed.

Middle neck and scrag end Relatively cheap and made tender by long, slow cooking.

Saddle of lamb Also called a double loin of lamb, this joint is too big to cook in a slow cooker.

Shoulder This roasting joint from the forequarter is fattier than the leg, so should be trimmed before pot-roasting on or off the bone. Boneless shoulder can be cubed for casseroles.

Noisettes and cutlets (below)

BELOW: *A small leg of lamb can be pot-roasted in the slow cooker; steaks cut from the leg are good for braises and casseroles. Tender noisettes cut from the rolled, boned loin are better suited to quick cooking, while lamb cutlets are great for braised dishes. Chump chops are good pan-fried or braised.*

Leg of lamb and leg steaks

Chump chops

Pork

This light meat is rich-tasting and very versatile. It is also good for slow cooking: whole joints can be pot-roasted, bacon and gammon can be poached, chops can be braised, and cubes of meat stewed. Pork products, such as sausages are fabulous cooked in hearty stews in the slow cooker.

Buying and storing

Pork should be a pale brownish-pink in colour with a smooth, moist, fine-grained texture. The fat should look white and firm.

Store pork on a low shelf in the refrigerator, below any food that will be eaten raw. Keep pre-packed meat in its packaging and observe the use-by dates. Minced (ground) pork can be kept for up to 2 days, while chops and joints can be kept for 3 days.

Classic flavourings
Pork is widely eaten in Europe, Asia and South and Central America. Because of its rich taste and texture, it goes well with fruity and acidic accompaniments. In England, Germany and France, apples are a popular choice, while in New England, cranberries are favoured. In other cuisines, peaches, apricots and pineapple are all used. Pungent herbs and spices are often added to pork dishes, and throughout Europe cabbage is a popular vegetable accompaniment.

CUTS OF PORK

Belly/side This cut can be rolled and tied to make a joint and pot-roasted.
Chops Large chump chops and leaner loin chops are good for braising.
Leg/ham Often weighing more than 4.5kg/10lb, this is too big for a slow cooker. However, it can be cut into two joints: the knuckle (shank) and the fillet. The knuckle can be pot-roasted. Leg steaks can be braised.
Neck end Cuts from this area include the spare rib, which is often cut into spare rib chops. They are good for braising.
Shoulder/blade This can be pot-roasted, but is usually trimmed, cubed and casseroled.
Tenderloin/fillet This lean, boneless piece of meat can be sliced into medallions or split lengthways, stuffed and tied.

BACON, HAM AND GAMMON

These are cured cuts of pork. Bacon is usually cured meat taken from the back and sides of the pig. Ham is the hind leg of a pig cut from the whole side, then cured separately. Gammon is the name of the whole hind leg cut from a side of bacon after curing. These joints respond well to poaching in the slow cooker, as long cooking makes them very tender. Strips of bacon are often fried in a pan before adding to slow cooker stews.

OFFAL

Known as variety meats in the United States, offal refers to the offcuts from an animal's carcass such as the organs, tail, head and feet. The heart, tongue and pig's trotters become deliciously tender when cooked in a slow cooker.

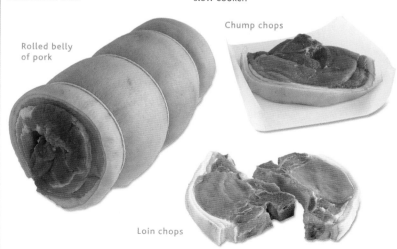

Rolled belly of pork

Chump chops

Loin chops

ABOVE: *Rolled belly of pork is perfect for pot-roasting in the slow cooker.*

ABOVE: *Loin chops (above) and chump chops (top) are very good for braising.*

Poultry and game

The term poultry covers domesticated birds, including chicken, turkey, duck, goose and guinea fowl, while game refers to wild birds and animals hunted for food, including pheasant, quail, wild rabbit and venison. However, many game birds and animals are now farmed.

Buying and storing

When buying fresh or chilled poultry, choose birds with soft blemish-free skin. Because poultry is susceptible to bacterial growth, keep poultry chilled. Place loose poultry in a deep dish and cover loosely, check pre-packed poultry to make sure that the packs are sealed and place on a plate, then store in the coldest part of the refrigerator. Check inside whole birds and remove any giblets. Always wash hands, utensils and surfaces after handling poultry.

When using frozen poultry, the safest way to thaw it is in the refrigerator. Once thawed or partially thawed, it should not be refrozen.

Store game birds in the coldest part of the refrigerator and use within 2 days of purchase or freeze at once. Before cooking wild game birds, rub your fingertips over the surface to locate any tiny balls of lead shot that may be left in them, then carefully cut them out with kitchen scissors or a filleting knife and discard.

SMALL POULTRY

Chicken is probably the most popular, but there are many other types that are just as good.

Poussin This is the French name for a young chicken, which is ideal for pot-roasting.

Spring chicken Sometimes called double poussins and will serve two.

Roasting chicken These can be pot-roasted whole or in portions, poached, braised or stewed.

Stewing or boiling chicken These birds are perfect for the slow cooker as they need slow simmering. Either poach or use for soups and stew.

Guinea fowl They respond best to pot-roasting, braising and stewing.

BELOW *(from left to right): Corn-fed, free-range and organic chickens are widely available.*

Jointing small poultry

This method of jointing can also be used for game birds, such as pheasant.

1 With the breast uppermost, use a sharp knife to remove the leg between the thigh and carcass. Cut, angling the knife inwards, through the ball and socket joint. Repeat with the other leg.

2 Using poultry shears, cut along the breastbone, between the breast sections. Turn the bird over and cut out the backbone. Using poultry shears, cut off the wing tips at the first joint.

3 Cut each breast section in half, leaving a portion of the breast attached to the wing. Next, cut each leg through the knee joint to separate the thigh and drumstick, making eight portions in all.

TURKEY

These substantial birds have dense meat that is lean and succulent. Whole birds won't fit in a slow cooker, but prepared joints and cuts are perfect for slow cooking.

DUCK

Flavourful, juicy and rich, duck is much fattier than chicken or turkey, with a higher proportion of bone to meat. The slow cooker is unsuitable for cooking whole birds, but duck breast portions can be used, providing the thick layer of fat is removed.

GAME BIRD

Pheasant For the best results, pot-roast or stew pheasants.
Grouse Young birds may be pot-roasted, but need to be kept moist with a layer of bacon over the breast.
Partridge Older birds should always be casseroled or braised.
Wild duck These are less fatty than farmed ducks, so cook smaller ones whole in a large slow cooker.
Pigeon Wild and wood pigeon can be stewed slowly to tenderize the meat.
Quail These are tiny and may be pot-roasted whole.

Pheasant

FURRED GAME

Game is cooked in the same way as other meats and recipes for similar types of meat are usually interchangeable. For example, wild boar can often be used instead of pork, farmed rabbit instead of chicken, and venison in place of beef in many recipes. Mature game should always be cooked using gentle, moist heat, such as braising and stewing, making it ideal for the slow cooker.
Deer Prime cuts, such as loin and fillet, are best roasted and served rare. Other cuts, such as shin, neck and shoulder, benefit from marinating then long and gentle cooking.
Wild boar It can be cooked in exactly the same way as pork, but care must be taken because the meat is dry and can easily become tough. Moist cooking methods work best.
Rabbit and hare The saddle of both can be roasted, but other cuts are best stewed. Boneless meat can be used in steamed puddings, terrines and pâtés.

Turkey

Duck

Pigeon

Rabbit

Quail

ABOVE: *The term poultry covers domesticated birds, including chicken, turkey, duck, goose and guinea fowl, while game refers to wild birds and animals hunted for food, including pheasant, pigeons, quail, wild ducks, such as mallards, hare and wild rabbit. However, many game birds and animals, such as quail, are often farmed.*

Hare

Fish and shellfish

The slow cooker is great for cooking fish and some shellfish, allowing the flavour to develop slowly and also helping to retain the fish's shape as it cooks. However, it is not suitable for cooking live shellfish, such as mussels and lobsters, because these require brief, fast boiling.

Buying and storing

Always buy the freshest fish and shellfish and cook it within 24 hours. There are many different ways to test the freshness of fish. Fish and shellfish should smell fresh; if it has an unpleasant fishy odour, it is past its best. The flesh should be elastic and firm to touch, if the body does not return to shape after being gently pressed with a finger then it is not as fresh as it should be. The eyes should also look bright and clear, not dry and cloudy. When buying shellfish, ensure that all of the shells are undamaged.

If you do not intend to use the fish within 24 hours of purchase, you should freeze the fish immediately. Most fish and shellfish from the supermarket have already been frozen, so shouldn't be refrozen, check this when you buy. In theory, fish can be kept frozen from 3 to 10 months depending on their oil content. However, fish loses flavour when frozen and so it is best to use it within a month of freezing.

Preparing round fish

This group includes white-fleshed fish such as cod, coley and haddock, and oily fish such as salmon and mackerel. Many are too big to be cooked whole in the slow cooker, so need to be sliced into steaks or filleted.

1 To remove the scales, place the fish on a sheet of newspaper. Scrape a fish scaler or knife against the skin, working from the tail to the head. Slit the fish open along the belly from the gills to the tail vent. Scrape out the innards, then rinse, inside and out. Cut off the head.

2 To fillet the fish, lay it carefully on its side, tail away from you. Using a sharp knife, make an incision along the backbone from the head to the tail, cutting through behind the gills. Starting at the head end, slide the knife carefully between the fillet and bones to release the fillet.

3 To skin the fillet, lay it skin side down. Using a sharp knife, make a cut at the tail end, cutting through the flesh, but not the skin, so that the fillet can be lifted away slightly. Hold the tail firmly with one hand and carefully "saw" the knife between the skin and the flesh.

Preparing flat fish

This group includes sole and plaice.

1 Place the fish, light side down, on a board. Make a cut down the centre following the backbone, then make a second cut round the head.

2 Slide the knife under one fish fillet, inserting the blade between the flesh and bones. Holding the loosened corner, cut the flesh from the bones. Remove the second fillet in the same way. Turn the fish over and repeat.

3 The skins are removed in the same way as above.

Preparing prawns/shrimp

Raw prawns may be cooked in their shells or peeled first. The dark intestinal vein is usually removed.

1 To peel, grip the head between your forefinger and thumb. Holding the body with your other hand, gently pull until the head comes off. Remove the legs and peel the shell from the body. The tail may be pulled away or left on.

2 To remove the dark intestinal vein, make a shallow cut down the centre of the back and pull out the vein using a knife blade.

Preparing squid

Unlike other shellfish, which have their protective shell on the outside, the shell of the squid is found inside its body.

1 Hold the body of the squid in one hand and the tentacles in the other and gently pull apart. Cut the tentacles away from the head just below the eyes and discard the head.

2 Remove the "quill" (the shell) and soft innards from the body and discard. Peel off the thin membrane, then rinse the body and tentacles under cold running water.

3 Slice the body into rings, or cut it into large pieces and lightly score in a criss-cross pattern.

COOKING FISH

Unlike meat, fish should be removed from the slow cooker as soon as it is done. It is ready when the flesh is still slightly translucent when eased away from the bone, and flakes easily. Poaching is a good method for cooking large, fairly firm pieces of fish, such as steaks or chunky fillets. It can also be used for small whole fish, while braising cooks the fish in a small amount of liquid.

Braising

1 Pour slightly less than 5mm/¼in white wine, cider or fish stock into the ceramic cooking pot and switch the slow cooker to high. Cover the pot with the lid.

2 Blend 25g/1oz butter with lemon or orange rind, salt and pepper.

Place four large, skinned lemon sole fillets on a chopping board and spread each with the butter.

3 To help protect the fillet during cooking, roll up the fillet, enclosing the filling, and place in the base of the cooking pot, with the loose end tucked underneath.

4 Sprinkle the fish with about 15ml/ 1 tbsp lemon juice. Cover the cooking pot and cook for 45 minutes–1½ hours, or until the fish is opaque and cooked through.

Poaching

1 Grease the base of the ceramic cooking pot. Place four 175–225g/ 6–8oz salmon fillets or similar in the base, leaving a little space between each one.

2 Pour over 150ml/¼ pint/²/₃ cup dry white wine and 300ml/½ pint/ 1¼ cups of boiling fish stock or water. Add a pinch of salt, 2 black peppercorns, a few onion slices, 1 bay leaf and a fresh parsley sprig.

3 Cover and switch the slow cooker to high. Cook for 45 minutes –1½ hours, or until cooked.

Vegetables

Cooking vegetables in the slow cooker is a good way to ensure they are tender without being overcooked, which can spoil their texture and subtle flavours.

Preparing vegetables

Many types of vegetables take longer to cook than meat in the slow cooker. To ensure that they cook within the recommended time, they should be cut into even-size pieces slightly smaller than the meat. When preparing onions, peel them and slice thinly or chop finely. Hard root vegetables such as carrots, potatoes, swedes (rutabagas) and turnips take the longest time to cook. Cut them into 5mm/¼in dice, slices or sticks and place them in the base of the cooker so they will be completely covered in liquid.

BELOW: *The onion family includes spring onions (scallions), red and white onions, and brown and banana shallots. Mushrooms have a distinctive taste and meaty texture.*

ONIONS

An essential ingredient in many slow cooker recipes, they take a long time to cook so are often fried in oil before adding to the slow cooker. Different types of onion have varying degrees of pungency: large, yellow onions are mild, while smaller, white onions have a stronger flavour. Leeks are part of the onion family and have a milder flavour than onions; they cook more quickly. Garlic adds flavour; the taste it imparts is milder when whole or sliced, and stronger when crushed or chopped. Slow cooking tames the pungency, so you may need to increase the amount in dishes cooked for more than 4 hours. Spring onions (scallions) are usually used raw, but have a delicate flavour when cooked.

ROOTS AND TUBERS

These vegetables, which include carrots, swedes (rutabagas), turnips, parsnips and potatoes, have a dense, sometimes starchy flesh. They take the longest time to cook in the slow cooker. Cut roots and tubers into pieces, no larger than 2.5cm/1in thick, and place in the base of the cooking pot, which is the hottest part during cooking. The vegetables should be immersed in the cooking liquid to ensure they soften, and to protect those roots and tubers, such as potatoes, that will discolour if exposed to air. In braised dishes that use a little liquid, you may need to layer the ingredients. If the dish contains ingredients that do not require long cooking, sauté the vegetables first.

MUSHROOMS

These add a deep colour and rich taste to many dishes. They give off a lot of liquid, so if you add extra mushrooms to a recipe, adjust the liquid content. Button mushrooms have a mild taste; small whole ones are good in casseroles. Flat mushrooms have a stronger flavour and are usually sliced or left whole and stuffed. Chestnut mushrooms have a darker brown skin, firmer texture and a stronger, nuttier taste than buttons. Delicate mushrooms, such as oyster and enoki, should be added to the slow cooker near the end of cooking. Dried mushrooms are used to thicken dishes by absorbing liquid. They should be pre-soaked in boiling water for a few minutes before adding, to remove any grit or dirt.

PUMPKINS AND SQUASHES

These come in many shapes, sizes and colours. Cooking in the slow cooker helps to develop their flavour and retain their firm texture. They tend to produce a lot of liquid during cooking, so don't add too much extra liquid to braised dishes containing pumpkins or squashes. Be careful not to overcook summer squashes, such as patty pans and courgettes (zucchini).

SHOOT VEGETABLES

This category covers a large number of vegetables, which vary widely in appearance and characteristics. Some, such as fennel, chicory and celery, respond well to slow cooking, while others, such as asparagus and globe artichokes, are better cooked using conventional methods.

VEGETABLE FRUITS

Although tomatoes, (bell) peppers and aubergines (eggplant) are all used as vegetables, botanically they are fruits.

Tomatoes Great for slow cooking, these add a rich colour and flavour to many dishes. They are juicy, so can be used as part of the cooking liquid. Long cooking can make the skins tough and seeds bitter, so these are best removed before cooking.

Sweet peppers Known as bell peppers in the United States, these come in many colours, including red, orange, yellow, green and purple. Green peppers tend to lose their colour and become bitter in slow cooked dishes, unless they are cut

into very small pieces and added towards the end of cooking. To make the most of their flavour, grill (broil) peppers until the skins are charred, then rub off and discard them.

Aubergines/eggplants
There are many types of aubergine, from large, glossy, dark-purple ones to the small, white egg-shaped ones. Very large aubergines may be slightly bitter, so should be salted after

slicing or cubing and left for half an hour, then rinsed well. This is also useful for drawing out liquid that would dilute the sauce of the dish.

BRASSICAS AND GREEN LEAFY VEGETABLES

Brassicas, such as broccoli and cauliflower, should be broken or cut into small sprigs to ensure they cook evenly in the slow cooker. When using leafy vegetables, such as cabbage and spinach, shred them very finely and always add to hot liquid so they cook in the shortest possible time to retain their taste and texture.

ABOVE: *(from left): Butternut, acorn and patty pan squashes are great in slow cooked dishes.*

Canned and frozen vegetables
These make a useful last-minute addition. Cooked, canned vegetables should be drained, then simply added 10 minutes before the end of cooking time. Frozen vegetables, such as peas and corn, should be defrosted first and need a little more cooking. Once added to the slow cooker they should be cooked for 15–20 minutes.

Grains, pasta and beans

Cereal grains, pasta and beans are all very versatile and can be used as a main ingredient or an accompaniment. Classic slow cooker dishes that use grains, pasta and beans as the main ingredient include risottos, pilaffs, lasagne, pasta bakes and bean stews and curries.

Buying and storing

Always buy dried beans, grains and pasta in small quantities from supermarkets that have a regular turnover to ensure that they have not been exposed to light for too long. Store beans and pulses in an airtight container away from the light and use them within 6–9 months of purchase. Uncooked rice can be stored in a cool, dark place for up to 3 years.

ABOVE: *Easy-cook brown rice is perfect for using in the slow cooker espcially when teamed with lime and lemon grass.*

RICE

Ordinary long grain rice doesn't cook very well in the slow cooker, but easy-cook (converted) rice gives excellent results. Also known as par-boiled rice, this type is soaked in water and then steamed under pressure, making it very difficult to overcook and lose all its nutrients. The grains remain separate during cooking and rarely become soggy or sticky, so it is particularly good for slow cooking, where the water bubbles very gently, if at all. The dry grains may appear more yellow than normal rice, but this coloration disappears during cooking, and when fully cooked the rice becomes bright white. You can buy easy-cook brown or wholegrain rice, easy-cook basmati rice, which is especially good for pilafs and Indian-style recipes, and easy-cook Italian risotto rice.

Making slow cooker rice

A savoury rice dish can be made easily in the slow cooker, and makes a good accompaniment for four people.

1 Grease the bottom of the cooking pot with 15g/$\frac{1}{2}$oz/1 tbsp butter, or 15ml/1 tbsp sunflower oil. Sprinkle over 4–6 finely chopped spring onions (scallions). Switch the cooker to high and cook for 20 minutes.

2 Add 1.5ml/$\frac{1}{4}$ tsp ground turmeric or a pinch of saffron strands and 750ml/1$\frac{1}{4}$ pints/3 cups boiling vegetable stock to the pot. If the stock is unseasoned, add a pinch of salt as well.

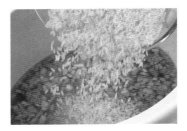

3 Sprinkle 300g/10oz/generous 1$\frac{1}{2}$ cups easy-cook rice over the stock and stir well. Cover and cook for about 1 hour, or until the rice is tender and plump and all the stock has been absorbed. Serve hot, or transfer into a shallow dish, stir in 30ml/2 tbsp vinaigrette, and serve warm or cold.

PASTA

Both ordinary and easy-cook pastas can be used successfully in the slow cooker. The latter gives the best results, but is not suitable for "all-day cooking"; the final result will be soft and soggy. As a general rule, pasta made from 100 per cent durum wheat holds its shape much better than the varieties made with eggs (*all'uova*). Fresh pasta is not suitable for use in slow cookers because it requires boiling in a large quantity of water. There is a wide range of shapes available, and the shape and size will affect the overall cooking times. Wholemeal (whole-wheat) pasta will take longer to cook than white pasta.

OTHER GRAINS

As well as rice, there are many other grains that can be cooked successfully in a slow cooker. Whole grains, such as barley, quinoa and whole wheat, can be served as an accompaniment instead of rice, pasta or potatoes, or as part of a main course. Whole rye grains need to be soaked in cold water overnight before they can be cooked. This is not necessary for most grains, although pre-soaking will shorten the cooking time.

Cooking grains

The cooking times vary from grain to grain; quinoa and millet take the least time, while grains such as barley and rye take much longer to cook. To speed up cooking and enhance the flavour, fry grains in a little oil for 2–3 minutes, before transferring to the slow cooker.

1 Allow about 75g/3oz per person for part of a main course. If the quantity of cooking liquid is not indicated on the packet, place the grains in a measuring jug (cup) to check their volume, then measure three parts boiling water or stock to one part grain (millet is the exception to this rule, and needs four parts water to one part grain).

2 Rinse the grains in a sieve (strainer) under cold running water, then place in the cooking pot and pour over the water or stock. Cover the cooking pot and cook on high for 40 minutes–2 hours, or until tender.

BEANS

The slow cooker was initially invented for the commercial cooking of baked beans, cooking haricot beans until they are perfectly tender, while still keeping their shape. The slow cooker is therefore great for cooking all types of dried beans, peas and lentils for use in a huge variety of slow-cooked dishes.

Cooking beans

Most beans, peas and lentils need to be soaked before cooking, but soaking times depend on the variety and also the age of the beans. Red lentils and split peas need no soaking; most beans should be soaked for at least 6 hours and some, such as chickpeas, for 8–12 hours. Beans should not be left to soak for more than 24 hours. When they are fully soaked, the skin should look plump and smooth.

1 Put the beans in a large bowl, cover with at least twice their volume of cold water and leave to soak for the required period of time.

2 Drain the beans, then rinse. Place the pulses in a large pan and pour over enough cold water to come 4cm/1½in above the beans. Bring to the boil and boil rapidly, uncovered, for 10–15 minutes. (All beans, except for lentils and gunga peas, should be boiled fast to destroy the toxins, then transfered to the slow cooker.)

3 Remove from the heat and skim off any froth on the surface. Leave to cool for 5 minutes, then transfer the beans and cooking liquid to the ceramic cooking pot. The liquid should cover the pulses by at least 2cm/¾in; if necessary, top up with a little boiling water.

4 Add flavouring ingredients, but do not add any salt or acidic ingredients – these will toughen the beans. Cover with the lid and cook on high for 1¼–5 hours. (Cooking times vary according to the type of bean: kidney beans take about 1½ hours and soya beans take 4½–5 hours. Canned beans need to be drained and added about 30 minutes before the end of the cooking time to allow them enough time to warm through.)

Fruit

The gentle simmering of the slow cooker makes it ideal for cooking all kinds of fruit to perfection. It is good for poaching delicate fruits that may break up during cooking, including soft fruits, such as currants and rhubarb. It can also be used to make desserts, such as crumbles.

Buying and storing

Choose fruit that looks fresh and avoid any with bruised or shrivelled skins. It is best to select fruit that is loose on the racks in supermarkets rather than prepackaged fruit, as this allows you to check all of them individually. Handle the fruit carefully to avoid bruising them. If any fruit does accidentally get bruised then it should be thrown away to prevent it rotting. It's best to buy locally produced fruit that is in season – you can be sure that it is fresh and it should be cheaper than fruit that is out of season.

Fruit should not be refrigerated until it has already ripened, otherwise it will not ripen properly. Fully ripened fruit and soft fruit should be eaten as soon as possible because they are very perishable. Keep ripe fruit such as peaches and cherries in the refrigerator if you are not ready to eat them, but bananas should be kept at room temperature (they spoil in temperatures below 13°C/55°F). Soft fruit will keep for just one or two days in the refrigerator.

PREPARING FRUIT

Many fruits need only simple preparation, such as washing, while others need to be peeled, cored, seeded or stoned (pitted) before they are cooked.

Peeling

Fruits such as apples, pears and peaches should be peeled before being cooked in a slow cooker.

To peel fruits such as apples and pears, use a vegetable peeler or a small paring knife to carefully pare off the skin in thin strips. It takes some practice, but apples can also be peeled in one single, spiral strip.

To peel fruits such as peaches and apricots, loosen the skins first. Make a nick in the skin using a small, sharp knife, then place in a heatproof bowl. Pour over enough boiling water to cover the fruits and leave for 20–30 seconds. Lift out using a small slotted spoon, rinse under cold water and the skin should peel off.

Coring

Tough cores, pips and stems should be removed from fruit before cooking so that they do not spoil the dish. When cooking chunks of fruit, first cut the fruit lengthways into quarters. Remove the core and pips, then peel and chop into smaller pieces.

Removing stones/pits

Hard stones should always be removed from fruit before cooking, since they will become loose as the fruit cooks.

To stone larger fruits such as plums and apricots, cut around the crease in the fruit. Twist the halves apart, then lever out the stone. To stone cherries, use a special cherry stoner.

COOKING FRUIT

Fruit can be cooked in all kinds of ways in a slow cooker, which is good for stewing and poaching, and can be used for "baking" as well.

Poaching and stewing

These techniques are slightly different. Poaching cooks fruit in a hot syrup, and is good for pears, stone fruits, and figs. Stewing is used for fruit such as apples, berries and rhubarb.

1 To stew rhubarb, cut 900g/2lb rhubarb into 2.5cm/1in pieces. Put into the ceramic cooking pot with 150–200g/5–7oz/³⁄₄–1 cup caster (superfine) sugar, sprinkling it between the layers. Pour over the juice of 1 large orange and 120ml/4fl oz/¹⁄₂ cup water.

2 Switch the slow cooker to high and cook for 1¹⁄₂ hours, or until the rhubarb is tender but still holds its shape. Stir halfway through cooking.

ABOVE: *Poaching apples and pears in a spicy wine syrup makes a delicious winter dessert for any occasion.*

Baked apples

To make baked apples, you can use either cooking or eating apples.

1 Keep the fruits whole, remove the cores with an apple corer, then using a sharp knife, carefully score the skin around the circumference.

2 Blend together 115g/4oz/¹⁄₂ cup soft light brown sugar and 50g/2oz/¹⁄₄ cup finely chopped dried fruit in a large bowl and use to fill the apples. Top each filled apple with a piece of butter and place in the ceramic cooking pot on a square of foil shaped to form a saucer.

3 Pour 150ml/¹⁄₄ pint/²⁄₃ cup very hot water carefully around the foil squares. Cover with the lid and cook on high for 2–3 hours, checking frequently. Remove the baked apples as soon as they are tender. Transfer to serving dishes and serve. They are excellent served with ice cream.

Making crumbles

Crumbles made in a slow cooker do not brown in the same way as crumbles made in a conventional oven, but using brown flour, oats, butter and crunchy sugar and a fairly dry fruit mixture gives similar results.

1 Combine prepared fruit such as apple and peach slices with a little sugar and 5ml/1 tsp cornflour (cornstarch). Add 30ml/2 tbsp fruit juice or water and switch the slow cooker to high.

2 Place 75g/3oz/³⁄₄ cup wholemeal (whole-wheat) flour and 50g/2oz/¹⁄₂ cup jumbo oats in a mixing bowl. Rub in 75g/3oz/6 tbsp butter. Stir in 50g/2oz/¹⁄₄ cup demerara (raw) sugar, then sprinkle over the fruit.

3 Cover with the lid and cook for about 3–4 hours, or until the fruit and topping are cooked, then serve.

Baking other fruits

Other fruits such as halved peaches and figs can be "baked" in the slow cooker, with just a tiny amount of liquid to start the cooking process.

To bake nectarines, figs and oranges, place the halved fruits in the buttered cooking pot. Sprinkle a little lemon juice and sugar over each one and dot with butter. Pour 75ml/5 tbsp water around the fruit, cover and cook on high for 1¹⁄₂–2 hours, or until tender.

Herbs

The judicious use of flavourings is the key to successful cooking. Some dishes require just a subtle hint, while others need more robust flavourings. Some flavourings can be added at the beginning of cooking but, in the case of tender fresh herbs and chillies they are added towards or at the end.

Buying and storing

While fresh herbs are usually considered superior, for slow cooker dishes dried herbs are often better as they have a stronger flavour, so they should be used more sparingly in dishes. Delicate fresh leaves lose their pungency and colour with long cooking, whereas dried herbs release their flavour slowly. As a general rule, fresh herbs should be added about 30 minutes before the end of cooking, or just before serving.

Buy dried herbs from a reliable source with a quick turnover and look for small packets. "Freeze dried" herbs have a good fresh flavour. Store dried herbs in airtight jars in a cool, dark place for up to 6–9 months. Try to buy fresh herbs on the day you need them. They will keep for several days sealed in a plastic bag and stored in the refrigerator. Bunches of herbs, such as parsley, which still have their roots intact can be stored in a jug (pitcher) of water with a plastic bag over their leaves in the refrigerator for a few days.

TENDER HERBS

These herbs have soft, fragile leaves and need careful handling. They should be added in the last few minutes of cooking time, or to the finished dish. Popular tender herbs include basil, chervil, dill, tarragon, mint, coriander (cilantro), lovage and the great all-rounder, parsley.

ABOVE:
Delicate dill has a mild aniseed flavour that goes well with fish.

ROBUST HERBS

These usually have tough, woody stems and pungent leaves and can withstand long cooking. They should be added at the start of cooking, then removed just before serving. Robust herbs include bay leaves, oregano, marjoram, thyme, rosemary, sage and kaffir lime leaves.

ABOVE: *Robustly flavoured rosemary and sage should be used sparingly.*

Making a bouquet garni

This simple bunch of herbs is a classic flavouring used in soups, casseroles and sauces.

Using a long piece of string, tie together a bay leaf with sprigs of parsley and thyme. When it is time to add the bouquet garni to the slow cooker, tie the string to the handle for easy removal.

Alternatively, place the herbs in a square of muslin (cheesecloth) and tie into a loose bag. Other herbs like rosemary and lemon thyme, or different flavourings, such as peppercorns, strips of orange rind, lemon zest, a sprig of celery leaves or even a sprig of fennel can also be added to suit an individual dish.

Spices and flavourings

Warm, fragrant spices are usually added at the start of cooking time. However, some may become bitter if cooked for many hours, and should be added partway through. Most spices are better used whole, rather than ground, in slow cooker dishes.

LEFT: *There are many different varieties of chilli.*

Buying and storing
Unless you will be using a particular spice frequently, it is normally best to buy small quantities frequently.

Store spices in a cool, dark place and check the sell-by date before using; they lose their taste and aroma with age. Whole spices will keep for up to a year; ground spices start to lose their pungency after 6 months. They should be kept in jars with air-tight lids.

ABOVE: *A wide variety of curry pastes is available or it is easy to make your own.*

HOT SPICES
Many spices add heat to dishes — some give just a hint of warmth, others a fierce heat. The main hot spices are chilli, ginger, pepper and mustard.

Fragrant spices
Some plants are grown for their fragrant, aromatic seeds. These are sold whole and ground. Long, slow cooking softens the whole seeds and releases their taste. Popular seed spices include cumin, coriander, caraway seeds and poppy seeds.

Spice mixtures
As well as individual spices, there are a number of ground spice mixes that are widely used in both sweet and savoury dishes. Popular mixes include mixed spice (apple pie spice), Chinese five-spice powder, garam masala and a wide variety of curry powders that vary in strength from mild to extremely hot. Jars of curry paste are also available.

OTHER FLAVOURINGS
As well as herbs and spices, there are many other flavourings that can be used to enliven dishes — ranging from pungent sauces to delicate flower waters, including rose water.

SAVOURY SAUCES
There are many savoury sauces that can be used to boost the flavour of dishes. They are strongly flavoured and often salty, so only a splash or two is required. Sauces include mushroom ketchup, Worcestershire sauce, dark and light soy sauce, hoisin and fish sauces, such as anchovy sauce, oyster sauce and *nam pla* (Thai fish sauce). They should be added at the beginning of cooking.

SWEET EXTRACTS
These have a rich, fragrant aroma and are used to flavour sweet dishes. You only need a little, sometimes just a few drops, to flavour a whole dish. Avoid artificial flavourings.

ALCOHOL
Because of the gentle heat, alcohol evaporates more slowly in a slow cooker, resulting in a stronger flavour. When adapting conventional recipes, the amount of alcohol should be reduced. Beer, cider and wine can be used in marinades and casseroles. Fortified wines, such as sherry can be used to enrich sweet and savoury dishes. Colourless fruit spirits, such as kirsch, and liqueurs, like amaretto, Grand Marnier and Drambuie can be used to flavour desserts.

Basic techniques: making stock

A good stock forms the foundation of many dishes, from simple soups and classic sauces to warming casseroles and pot-roasts. Making your own stock is very easy and inexpensive.

Types of stock

There are two types of stock: brown stock, where the vegetables and bones are roasted in the oven first, and white stock, where the ingredients are only boiled. Clean vegetable peelings, celery leaves and the stalks from fresh herbs are useful additions, providing extra flavour. Always start making a stock with cold water any vegetables should be at room temperature. Use whole peppercorns because long cooking times make ground pepper taste bitter.

ABOVE: *The ingredients used for stock can be varied according to what is available.*

Making meat stock

Used for meat dishes, such as casseroles, and as a base for light soups, basic meat stock is traditionally made from veal bones. Beef bones will also make a good stock but with a stronger flavour. Lamb bones may also be used, but this stock can only be used for lamb dishes. Some recipes include lean stewing meat, such as shin of beef, which gives a much meatier flavour. For this option, you will need 450g/1lb each bones and meat

MAKES ABOUT 1.2 LITRES/ 2 PINTS/5 CUPS

675g/1¹/₂lb beef or veal bones
1 onion, unpeeled and quartered
1 carrot, sliced
1 celery stick, sliced
6 black peppercorns
1 fresh bouquet garni
about 1.2 litres/2 pints/5 cups
   cold water

1 Using a meat cleaver, carefully chop any large bones, so that they will fit snugly into the slow cooker. (Cutting the bones into several pieces will also increase the flavour of the finished stock.)

2 Place all the vegetables in the ceramic cooking pot. Add the peppercorns and the bouquet garni, then place the bones on top, packing them in tightly so that they fit in a single layer on top of the vegetables and herbs.

3 Pour over the water, adding a little more, if necessary, to cover the bones, but leaving a space of at least 4cm/1¹/₂in between the water and the top of the pot. Cover and cook on high or auto for 2 hours.

4 Using a slotted spoon, skim off any scum and turn the temperature to low or leave on auto and cook for 5 hours.

5 Strain the stock through a fine sieve (strainer) and leave to cool. This should be done quickly, ideally over a bowl of iced water. Cover the stock and leave to chill in the refrigerator for at least 4 hours, then remove the fat from the surface.

Making fish stock

This light broth can be used as the base for delicate fish soups and hearty stews, as well as for poaching. It is the quickest and most easily made of all stocks. Unlike other stocks, fish stock should not be simmered for very long, otherwise it will become bitter. Once the stock has come to simmering point (which will take about 1 hour), it should be kept at a bare simmer for no more than 1 hour.

MAKES ABOUT 900ML/
1¹/2 PINTS/3³/4 CUPS

900g/2lb fish bones and trimmings
2 carrots, finely sliced
1 onion, sliced
6 white peppercorns
1 bouquet garni
900ml/1¹/2 pints/3³/4 cups water

1 Rinse all the fish bones and trimmings well under cold running water and, using a sharp knife, cut any larger bones or pieces into several chunks so that they will easily fit inside the ceramic cooking pot. For a fish stock, use the bones and trimmings from white fish, such as sole or plaice; you can also include prawn (shrimp) heads and tails.

2 Arrange the vegetables in the base of the cooking pot. Sprinkle over the peppercorns, add the bouquet garni and place the fish bones on top.

3 Pour the cold water into the pot, adding a little more to cover the bones, if necessary, but leaving a space of 4cm/1¹/2in between the water and the top of the cooking pot. Cover, then cook on high or auto for 1 hour until simmering.

4 Skim off any scum that has risen to the surface. Reduce the temperature to low or leave on auto, re-cover and cook for 1 hour. (Do not cook for longer than this.)

5 Using a fine sieve (strainer) pour the stock into a bowl, then cool quickly, ideally in a bowl of iced water. Cover and store in the refrigerator, or freeze.

Making vegetable stock

You can vary the vegetables used in this recipe, but be sure to wash them well and chop fairly small. Strong-tasting vegetables, such as turnips and parsnips, should be used in small quantities; their flavour will dominate otherwise. Starchy vegetables, such as potatoes, should be avoided; they will make the stock cloudy.

MAKES ABOUT 1.5 LITRES/
2¹/2 PINTS/6¹/4 CUPS

1 large onion, unpeeled and chopped
1 leek, roughly chopped
2 carrots, thinly sliced
1 celery stick, thinly sliced
2 bay leaves
1 sprig fresh thyme
a few fresh parsley stalks
6 white peppercorns
about 1.5 litres/2¹/2 pints/
    6¹/4 cups water

1 Put the vegetables, herbs and peppercorns in the ceramic cooking pot and pour over the water. Cover and cook on high or auto for 2 hours.

2 Using a slotted spoon, skim off any scum that rises to the surface. Reduce the temperature to low, or leave on auto, and cook for 2 hours.

3 Strain the stock through a fine sieve (strainer) into a bowl and cool. Cover and store in the refrigerator, or freeze. Always make sure that any stock, whether it is vegetable, fish or meat, is brought to the boil before using. If you don't have time to make your own, use ready-made ones.

Making stews and casseroles

The slow cooker's gentle heat makes it perfect for stews and casseroles. The lengthy cooking allows all cuts of meat to become tender, and even the toughest can be turned into a delicious meal.

What are stews and casseroles?

Stews, casseroles, carbonnades, hot-pots and navarins are all names for what is, essentially the same type of dish. The word stew once described dishes cooked on the stovetop, while casserole described dishes cooked in the oven, but now the names are largely interchangeable.

Choosing the right cut

Ideal meats for slow cooking are the cheaper cuts, such as brisket, chuck steak, blade-bone, shank and knuckle. These cuts come from the part of the animal (usually the front) that has worked hardest, so have a looser texture and a good marbling of fat. These cuts also have far greater flavour than very lean ones.

ABOVE: *Provençal beef stew*

Preparing meat

Tougher cuts of meat cook more evenly and quickly if they are cut into small, even-size cubes. Although excess fat should be removed, some marbling is useful for keeping the meat moist. Any excess fat can be skimmed off after cooking.

1 Trim the meat, cutting off all the excess fat and any gristle, sinew or membranes while it is in one piece. Cut the meat across the grain into 2.5cm/1in thick slices. Cutting across the grain makes the meat more tender when it is cooked for longer.

2 To cut the meat into cubes, first cut the slices lengthways into thick strips. Remove any excess fat or gristle as you go, then cut each strip crossways into 2.5cm/1in cubes. Make sure that all the cubes are roughly the same size so they all cook at the same rate.

Preparing chops

These are usually sold ready-prepared and fairly lean, but it is usually worth trimming the fat a little before cooking. This will help them cook, look and taste better.

1 Using sharp kitchen scissors or a sharp knife, remove the excess fat from the edge of the chop by cutting around the contours of the chop. Do not remove the fat completely, leave a little less than 5mm/1/4in fat on the edge of each chop.

2 If you are going to pre-fry chops before adding to the slow cooker, make shallow cuts all around the edge. The edge of the meat will then fan out during frying, preventing the meat curling up, so that it stays in constant contact with the frying pan.

Preparing poultry

A variety of chicken and game portions can be used in stews and casseroles – from whole or diced breast portions, to drumsticks and thighs. Generally, it is better to remove poultry skin before casseroling because it won't crispen during the moist cooking.

To skin breast fillets, carefully pull the skin and thin membrane away from the meat. If you like, use a small, sharp knife to cut the meat off the rib bone and any remaining breastbone. Turn the breast portion over and remove the thin, white central tendons from the meat.

To prepare escalopes (scallops), cut the breast in half horizontally, holding your hand on top of the chicken breast as you cut. A chicken breast portion will yield two escalopes, a duck breast portion four, and a turkey breast portion should yield at least four.

To skin chicken thighs, use a knife to loosen the skin, then pull it away from the meat. To bone the thighs, carefully cut the flesh lengthways along the main thigh bone, using a boning knife or a small, sharp knife, then cut the bone out, trimming the meat close to it.

Thickening stews

There are various ways to thicken the sauces of stews and casseroles.

Cornflour/cornstarch or arrowroot These very fine flours can both be used as thickeners. They should be blended with a little water or other cold liquid before being stirred into the stew.
Flour Meat is often fried first, and can be first dusted in flour, which will act as a thickener for the juices as the meat cooks. Do not over-brown the flour as this gives it a bitter flavour; only fry until light brown. Alternatively, you can add flour

ABOVE: *To thicken a stew you can whisk in a paste made from equal quantities of flour and butter.*

towards the end of cooking time by whisking in a paste made from equal quantities of flour and butter. Allow extra cooking time to allow the flour to cook and lose its "raw" flavour.
Pasta and rice If it becomes obvious part-way through cooking that the stew or casserole will be too thin, you can stir in a little pasta or easy-cook (converted) rice, which will absorb some of the liquid. These should be added about 45 minutes before the end of cooking time. (Lentils and grains, such as pearl barley, will also act as thickeners, but these must be added early in the cooking time to cook thoroughly.)
Reduction If the sauce is too thin when cooking is complete, lift out the meat and vegetables with a slotted spoon and set aside. Pour the liquid into a wide pan and boil fast to reduce the liquid. Add the meat and vegetables and gently reheat.

Making savoury sauces

Sauces add flavour, colour, texture and moisture to food. Many can be made in the slow cooker, from classic sauces to emulsions, such as hollandaise, that are made by using the cooker as a bain-marie (a device where the vessel containing food is set in a larger vessel holding warm water, to allow for slow and even cooking). Here are a selection of sauces that can be used for cooking or for serving with other dishes.

Making fresh tomato sauce

This sauce can be used as the base for many pasta dishes, or it can be combined with meat or poultry to make a rich cooking sauce. You can use 2 x 400g/14oz cans chopped plum tomatoes instead of the fresh tomatoes, if you prefer. This recipe will make about 475ml/16fl oz/2 cups of tomato sauce.

1 Pour 15ml/1 tbsp olive oil into the pot. Add 2 crushed garlic cloves and the finely grated zest of ¹/₂ lemon. Stir, then cover and switch the slow cooker to high. Cook for 15 minutes.

2 Peel and roughly chop 900g/2lb ripe tomatoes and add to the cooking pot with 60ml/4 tbsp vegetable stock or red wine, 5ml/1 tsp dried oregano and a pinch of caster (superfine) sugar. Stir to combine, then cover with the lid and cook on low for 3 hours.

3 Stir in 30–45ml/2–3 tbsp chopped fresh basil and season to taste with salt and ground black pepper.

Making white sauce

To make white sauce in a slow cooker, heat the milk, then whisk in a mixture of butter and flour. This recipe will make about 475ml/16fl oz/2 cups.

1 Pour 400ml/14fl oz/1²/₃ cups milk into the ceramic cooking pot. Add your chosen flavouring ingredients (such as a bay leaf or two, a blade of mace, a few fresh parsley stalks, half a peeled onion and 4 black peppercorns). Switch the slow cooker to high and heat for about 1 hour, or until the milk mixture is gently simmering.

2 Blend 20g/³/₄oz/1¹/₂ tbsp softened butter with 20g/³/₄oz/ scant ¹/₄ cup plain (all-purpose) flour in a bowl to make a paste. This is a roux-based sauce, which is the most familiar type. White béchamel

sauce is one of the classics and the roux or butter and flour mixture is cooked but not coloured. For a velouté, the roux is cooked until it is coloured.

3 Remove the flavouring ingredients from the cooking pot using a slotted spoon. Add the paste in small spoonfuls and whisk into the hot milk until the mixture thickens.

4 Cover with the lid and cook for about 30 minutes, stirring occasionally. Season with salt and extra pepper if needed.

Making a sabayon sauce

Light and airy sabayon sauce is thickened with egg. It goes well with vegetable and pastry dishes. This recipe will make about 300ml/$\frac{1}{2}$ pint/ 1$\frac{1}{4}$ cups.

1 Half-fill the cooking pot with near-boiling water, cover with the lid and switch the slow cooker to high. You can also make a sweet sabayon sauce with 4 eggs, 50g/2oz/$\frac{1}{4}$ cup caster (superfine) sugar and 100ml/3$\frac{1}{2}$fl oz/generous $\frac{1}{3}$ cup sweet wine. This makes 450ml/$\frac{3}{4}$ pint/scant 2 cups.

2 Place a heatproof bowl over the water in the slow cooker; the base should just touch the water but the rest of the bowl should be above the water. Place 4 egg yolks with 15ml/ 1 tbsp white wine vinegar in the bowl and whisk until pale. Add 90ml/6 tbsp wine or stock and whisk again.

3 When the sauce is thick and frothy, season to taste with salt and freshly ground black pepper and serve with the dish of your choice. This sauce needs to be used immediately as the airiness created by the whisking of the egg yolk mixture collapses after about 30 minutes.

Making hollandaise sauce

This rich sauce goes well with shellfish, fish and many vegetables. This recipe will make 300ml/$\frac{1}{2}$ pint/1$\frac{1}{4}$ cups.

1 About 30 minutes before making the sauce, remove 150g/5oz/$\frac{3}{4}$ cup unsalted (sweet) butter from the refrigerator. Cut into tiny cubes and leave to come to room temperature.

2 Pour about 5cm/2in near-boiling water into the ceramic cooking pot. Cover the slow cooker with the lid to retain the heat and switch to high.

3 Put 60ml/4 tbsp white wine vinegar in a pan with 4 black peppercorns and 1 bay leaf. Bring to the boil and simmer until reduced to 15ml/1 tbsp. Remove from the heat and dip the base of the pan into cold water.

4 Beat 3 egg yolks with 15g/$\frac{1}{2}$oz/ 1 tbsp of the butter and a pinch of salt in a heatproof bowl that will fit in the slow cooker. Strain in the reduced vinegar. Place the bowl in the cooking pot and pour enough boiling water around the bowl to come just over halfway up the sides. Whisk for about 3 minutes until beginning to thicken.

5 Beat in the remaining butter a little at a time, making sure that each addition of butter is completely incorporated before adding the next. The mixture will slowly thicken and emulsify. Season with salt and ground black pepper. Switch the slow cooker to low and keep the hollandaise warm for up to 1 hour.

Making beurre blanc

This simple butter sauce is served with poached or grilled (broiled) fish and poultry. It can be varied by adding chopped fresh herbs, such as chives or chervil, to the finished sauce. This will make about 250ml/8fl oz/1 cup.

1 Pour about 5cm/2in of near-boiling water into the cooking pot. Cover with the lid and switch the slow cooker to high.

2 Pour 45ml/3 tbsp each of white wine and white wine vinegar into a pan. Add 2 finely chopped shallots and bring to the boil. Simmer until the mixture is reduced to about 15ml/ 1 tbsp liquid.

3 Strain the mixture through a sieve into a heatproof bowl that will fit inside the slow cooker, then carefully pour enough boiling water around the bowl to come halfway up the sides.

4 Whisk in 225g/8oz/1 cup chilled diced butter, adding it piece by piece and making sure that each addition is completely incorporated before adding the next. Season with salt and freshly ground black pepper and serve with fish or chicken.

Making sweet sauces

A sweet sauce adds the finishing touch to a dessert, and the slow cooker is excellent for making delicious fruit purées, coulis, creamy custards, sweet sabayon sauces and rich white and plain dark chocolate sauces to accompany any number of different hot and cold desserts. If you intend to serve any of these sauces with a hot dessert that is made in a slow cooker, you may need to reheat the dessert or keep it warm in a low oven while you cook the sauce.

Making fresh fruit coulis

Cooking soft fruits, such as raspberries, blackberries, blueberries, blackcurrants, plums, cherries and apricots, brings out their natural flavour. This recipe will make about 350ml/12fl oz/1½ cups.

1 Put 350g/12oz/3 cups prepared fruit in the ceramic cooking pot with 45ml/3 tbsp water. Stir in a little sugar and add a dash of lemon juice. Cover with the lid and cook on high for 1–1½ hours or until very soft.

2 Remove the cooking pot from the slow cooker and leave to cool slightly. Pour the fruit into a food processor or blender and process until smooth.

3 Press the purée through a sieve (strainer) to remove any seeds or skins. Taste the sauce and stir in a little more sugar or lemon juice, if needed. Cover and chill until required. If you like, stir in 45ml/3 tbsp liqueur, such as Kirsch, before serving. The coulis can be stored in the refrigerator for up to 5 days.

Making custard

Custard is the classic dessert sauce and can also be used as the basis for many different desserts. The slow cooker maintains a gentle, constant heat, so the custard can be made directly in the cooking pot. This will make about 600ml/1 pint/2½ cups. When making custard do not overheat the mixture or cook it for too long otherwise the egg will set and separate out from the liquid. For best results make sure the eggs are well whisked. The custard can be used immediately, left to cool and served cold or used as part of another recipe.

1 Pour 475ml/16fl oz/2 cups of milk into the ceramic cooking pot. Using a small sharp knife, split a vanilla pod (bean) lengthways and add it to the milk. Switch the slow cooker to high and heat for about 1 hour, or until the milk just reaches boiling point.

2 Meanwhile, using a small balloon whisk, whisk together 5 egg yolks and 90g/3½ oz/scant ½ cup

caster (superfine) sugar in a medium-sized bowl until the mixture is pale and thick. Whisk 5ml/1 tsp cornflour

(cornstarch) into the egg mixture. This will help the custard achieve a more appetizing thickened consistency.

3 Remove the vanilla pod and pour the hot milk over the egg mixture, whisking. Pour the mixture back into the cooking pot and stir until slightly thickened. Bring to simmering point; do not let it boil or it may curdle. Cook until it is thick enough to coat the back of a wooden spoon.

Making butterscotch sauce

This buttery sauce is very sweet and rich and should be served in small quantities.

1 Put 50g/2oz/¼ cup unsalted (sweet) butter, 75g/3oz/6 tbsp soft light brown sugar, 50g/2oz/¼ cup caster (superfine) sugar and 150g/5oz/scant ½ cup golden (light corn) syrup into the ceramic cooking pot. Switch the slow cooker to high and heat for 20 minutes, stirring constantly, until the sugar has completely dissolved.

2 Gradually stir in 150ml/¼ pint/⅔ cup double (heavy) cream and 5ml/1 tsp vanilla extract. Serve the butterscotch warm with the dessert of your choice.

Making creamy chocolate sauce

This dark, luxurious and velvety smooth sauce should be served with desserts that can stand up to its rich flavour.

1 Pour 200ml/7fl oz/scant 1 cup double (heavy) cream, 60ml/4 tbsp milk and 2.5ml/½ tsp vanilla extract into the cooking pot. Switch the slow cooker to high and heat for about 45 minutes.

2 Turn off the slow cooker. Add 150g/5oz chopped dark (bittersweet) chocolate and stir continuously until it has melted. Serve warm.

Making caramel sauce

This rich, creamy sauce is delicious poured over sweet pastries and pastry desserts.

1 Put 25g/1oz/2 tbsp unsalted (sweet) butter and 75g/3oz/6 tbsp soft dark brown sugar in the pot. Switch the slow cooker to high and heat for 20 minutes, stirring occasionally, until the butter has melted and the sugar has dissolved.

2 Stir 150ml/¼ pint/⅔ cup double (heavy) cream into the sauce and cook for 20 minutes, stirring occasionally, until smooth.

Making glossy chocolate sauce

This sweet pouring sauce is perfect for serving with profiteroles and vanilla ice cream.

1 Put 225g/8oz chopped plain (semisweet) chocolate, 60ml/4 tbsp golden (light corn) syrup, 60ml/4 tbsp water and 25g/1oz/2 tbsp unsalted (sweet) butter into the ceramic cooking pot.

2 Switch the slow cooker to high and heat, stirring, for 30 minutes until melted. Serve warm with a dessert of your choice or even just with a scoop or two of vanilla ice cream.

ABOVE: *Chocolate chip and banana pudding with glossy chocolate sauce.*

Slow cooker safety

The slow cooker is an extremely efficient and safe way to cook food. It is however an electrical appliance, and some basic common-sense safety precautions should be followed. Because slow cooker models vary, always take the time to read the instruction manual supplied by the manufacturer before using your slow cooker.

ABOVE: *Protect your hands from the hot cooker and escaping steam with a pair of padded oven gloves.*

ABOVE: *Do not submerge the slow cooker in water. If it needs cleaning, make sure it is unplugged and use a damp, soapy sponge.*

Cooker care

Looking after your cooker is simple but very important. Before you use the slow cooker for the first time, wash the ceramic cooking pot in warm soapy water and dry it thoroughly. Stand the slow cooker on a heat-resistant surface when in use; the slow cooker should not touch anything hot or hang over the edge of the table or work-top in case it falls off accidentally.

• Take extra care if you have young children (or curious pets) and position the slow cooker out of reach. After an hour or so of cooking, the slow cooker can become very hot; not just the ceramic cooking pot, but the outer casing and the lid as well. Always use oven gloves when lifting the lid, and when removing the cooking pot from inside the slow cooker.

• Do not switch on the slow cooker if the ceramic cooking pot is empty (the only exception to this would be if the manufacturer recommends preheating). As soon as you have finished cooking, always remove the plug from the socket to prevent the slow cooker being switched on accidentally.

• Never immerse the outer casing of the slow cooker in water because the outer casing contains the electrical elements that heat the ceramic cooking pot.

• You should never use the outer casing for cooking without the ceramic cooking pot in place. If you need to clean the casing, do so carefully with warm soapy water and a damp cloth, and be sure that the appliance is unplugged before you put it in contact with water.

Ensuring food safety

Slow cookers cook food slowly using a gentle heat – the precise temperature will vary from model to model but the average is from about 90°C/200°F on the low setting to about 150°C/300°F on the high setting. Bacteria in food is destroyed at a temperature of 74°C/165°F, so as long as the food is cooked for the appropriate length of time, as stated in the recipe, this temperature will be reached quickly enough to ensure that the food is safe to eat. However, additional factors may affect the slow cooker's ability to reach the desired temperature:

• Avoid placing the slow cooker near an open window or in a draught.

• Do not lift the lid during cooking time unless instructed to do so in the recipe.

• Do not add ingredients that are frozen or part-frozen to the ceramic cooking pot because they will increase the length of time needed to reach the required cooking temperature, and the timings given in the recipe will not be sufficient.

• Increase the cooking time in extreme cold temperatures, where the kitchen temperature is considerably lower than normal, and check food is thoroughly cooked through and is piping hot before serving, particularly if cooking poultry and pork.

ABOVE: *A skewer or the tip of a sharp knife can be inserted into a thick part of a meat joint to check that it is cooked*

Checking meat is cooked

When it comes to food safety, one of the main things to look out for is that meat is properly cooked – in particular, poultry and pork. A meat thermometer is a worthwhile investment if you are planning to cook whole joints of meat and poultry in your slow cooker.

To check that meat is cooked without a thermometer, insert the tip of a thin sharp knife or skewer into the thickest part of the meat joint and hold it there for 20 seconds. For medium to well-cooked lamb or beef, the juices will be almost clear and the knife or skewer will feel hot on the back of the hand.

When cooking pork or poultry, it is essential that the meat juices should be completely clear. If there is any trace of pink, the meat is not ready to eat and should be cooked for a further 30 minutes; check again with the skewer or knife before serving. With poultry, you can double check by giving the leg a gentle tug – it should have some give in it and not be resistant.

Food safety tips

Basic food safety recommendations should be followed when preparing or using food in the slow cooker.

- Food should always be at room temperature when it is added to the slow cooker, However, ingredients such as meat and fish should not be left out of the refrigerator for longer than is necessary, so remove from the refrigerator just to take off the chill and keep covered.
- Marinating food in the ceramic cooking pot before cooking saves on washing up, but the cooking pot will become cold in the refrigerator, so remove it at least 1 hour before you plan to start cooking.

- Large joints of meat and whole poultry should be cooked at a high temperature for the first 1–2 hours to accelerate the cooking process. Switch the slow cooker to low for the remaining cooking time. This helps to ensure that it is thoroughly cooked.

- Avoid lifting the lid of the ceramic cooking pot during the cooking time, especially in the early stages. It takes 15–20 minutes to recover the lost heat each time the lid is removed, so it will take much longer to reach a safe temperature.
- Don't be tempted to partially cook meat or poultry, then refrigerate for subsequent cooking. Also avoid reheating pre-cooked dishes in the slow cooker.
- Frozen foods should always be thoroughly thawed before cooking in the slow cooker. If added when frozen, they will increase the time the food takes to reach a safe temperature. If adding frozen vegetables towards the end of cooking time, thaw them first under cold running water.
- Soak dried beans, in particular red kidney beans, overnight in a large bowl of water. The next day, drain the beans and then fast-boil them on the stovetop for 10 minutes in a large saucepan of fresh cooking water to destroy all the toxins before adding to the slow cooker. Check the packaging if in doubt.

Index